An
Ocean East
Teaching
Publication

The Scorpion Files

Lies Satan Tells . . . to Young Catholics

Michelle Willis
and
Jackie Cole

OCEAN EAST PUBLISHING

THE SCORPION FILES
by Michelle Willis and Jackie Cole

ISBN: 0-9607028-5-7
Library of Congress No.: 96-68758
Price: $12.00

Copyright © 1997 by Michelle Willis and Jackie Cole

Cover and Interior Design by Rainbow Books, Inc.

Published by Ocean East Publishing
1655 - 71st Court
Vero Beach, FL 32966
Telephone (561) 567-6050

Scripture excerpts taken from *The New American Bible*, Catholic Bible Publishers, 1970.

Printed in the United States of America.

DEDICATION

To our mothers, Irene and Teresa
for their precious lessons
of lived faith
and to our many students
over the years
who made sharing our
faith journey with them
a blessing.

Contents

– The Letters –

Contents

9

Foreword

Back in the 1980s, George Gallup conducted a survey in which he concluded that most teenagers were unable to give the Ten Commandments; that 20 percent of those who attended religious services regularly did not know what Easter commemorates. The survey also showed that only one-third of all the teens surveyed plus one half of those who attend church services on Sunday were able to name the authors of the four Gospels. The Church is facing the reality of massive ignorance of the truths of our Catholic faith.

Pope John Paul II has repeatedly said that the modern world has lost its sense of sin. Watching television today would certainly give plentiful evidence of this sad and painful fact. Children coming from homes where there is little or no faith formation are particularly vulnerable. Since our public school system has identified ethical morality with religion, moral teaching is lacking in the curriculum. Presently, there is little moral formation coming from our public schools.

There is an apathy among adolescents today to learn about their faith. Coupled with this apathy there is a major lack of religious literacy present among them. As a result of this chaotic situation, they base their beliefs on what the media presents as acceptable. The acceptable morality among so many young people is "whatever feels good is okay; my body is my own and no one can tell me what to do or how to behave, etc."

Any tool that will make catechesis attractive while preserving the Church's orthodox teachings is a most welcome asset. Such a tool is Michelle Willis and Jackie Cole's book titled: *The Scorpion Files*. It is written in the tradition of C.S. Lewis' *Screwtape Letters* and is designed to excite the curiosity of young people regarding questions of morality which are treated in the letters exchanged between Scorpion, an experienced demon, and his trainee, Agent 6. It has been used at St. John of the Cross in a senior catechetical class with great success.

Among the topics treated are the Church, the Sacrifice of the Mass, the sacraments, sin, the Commandments, prayer, the occult, and the Blessed Virgin Mary. These topics are presented in an engaging, interesting way that challenges each young person to come to know and appreciate the Church's teaching. *The Scorpion Files* is an effective treatment of catechetical material for today's youth.

Rev. John A. Crowley,
Pastor
St. John of the Cross Parish
Vero Beach, Florida

A Special Note

In each chapter you will find that certain terms are in **bold print**. Each of these **bold print** terms is included in the Glossary of Terms in the back of the book. You may be familiar with some of these terms, while others may need further explanation. To gain a thorough understanding of this material, it will be helpful for you to check the meanings of all the **bold print** terms, but especially those with which you are not familiar.

A Fable

A scorpion, being a very poor swimmer, once asked a turtle to carry him on his back across a river. "Are you mad?" exclaimed the turtle. "You'll sting me while I'm swimming and I'll drown."

The scorpion laughed as he replied, "My dear turtle, if I were to sting you, you would drown and I would go down with you. Now, what would be the point of that? I won't sting you. It would mean my own death."

The turtle thought about the logic of his argument for a few moments and then said, "You're right. Hop on!" The scorpion climbed aboard and halfway across the river, he gave the turtle a mighty sting.

As the turtle began to sink to the bottom of the river with the scorpion on its back, it moaned in dismay, "After your promise, you still stung me! Why did you do that? Now, we're both doomed."

The drowning scorpion replied, "I couldn't help it. **It's my nature to sting.**"

Introduction

Dear Reader,

There is no doubt that **Satan** would not want you to read these highly confidential letters, but because the information they contain could make the difference in your choice between eternal life and eternal death, you will naturally want to know the secrets they contain. The following information will assist you in grasping the significance of what these letters reveal.

A spirit is a being that has understanding and free will, but no physical body. A spirit is eternal; it never dies. Angels are spirits. When God created the angels, He gave to them great gifts of wisdom, power, and holiness. These angelic creations, or pure spirits, were created by God in great numbers and arranged in **"choirs."** They were created to constitute God's court of honor in Heaven. Angels were also brought into existence to serve God in various ways, especially as His ministers. God has often made His will known through the angels, as He did, for example, on the occasion of the Annunciation, when Mary was told that she was to be the Mother of God, also at the birth of Jesus, when the angels appeared to the shepherds, and again after Christ's Resurrection, when the angel announced to the holy women that Jesus had risen.

God also created the angels to be the guardians of human souls. We are each entrusted to the guidance and protection of an angel. Our personal **Guardian Angel** never abandons us, but is ever present with us to protect us from harm and to inspire us to do good. Because our Guardian Angel is an ever-present trustworthy guide and companion, God commands us to honor him, to listen to him when he inspires us to do good, and to invoke him often in times of danger and temptation.

However, not all of the angels which God originally created remained "good." They were not all faithful to God's Will. Some of them sinned. They aligned themselves with a particularly bright and beautiful angel named Lucifer, who was very proud and dared to rebel against God. As a result of Lucifer's rebellion, he was removed from his honorable and exalted position and cast into **Hell**. The angels who gave their allegiance to Lucifer instead of God were also cast into Hell. Lucifer has been assigned the name Satan, and the unfaithful angels who followed him are referred to as demons.

Demons, because they were first created by God as angels, are spirits without a body, but with understanding and free will. As a result of their rebellion and subsequent exile, they have taken upon themselves, not the role of being the ministers of God as they were created to be, but rather, the role of God's enemies. No longer able to take revenge on God directly, Satan and his demons are determined to try in every way to harm God's children instead. The demons actually envy human souls because they are destined to occupy the places in Heaven which Satan and his followers forfeited by their rebellion.

One cannot exaggerate the malice and fury of Satan and his demons against God and against mankind. They promote every variety of vice and sin. They cultivate lies and false teachings, and they continually advance erroneous ideas which lure people away from the true path of eternal life, which is through God's Son, Jesus Christ, and through His Church.

The author of these letters, known only by his code name *Scorpion*, is an experienced deceiver. His correspondence is with a less experienced demon, Agent 6, to whom *Scorpion* has been assigned as supervisor and trainer. Satan and his demons want to claim you for their own, and in these letters you will discover just how they plan to accomplish their evil designs. Having been made aware of this, you will want to read these letters with careful attention. Keep in mind, however, that Satan would not want you to know the deadly secrets these letters contain.

The
Letters

Letter 1

Dear Agent 6,

Congratulations on your appointment as chief agent in charge of that group of our Enemy's followers known as Catholic youth. You have undertaken an assignment of immense importance in the eyes of Satan – the Father of Darkness. The potential of your new assignment for misguiding young souls is very promising, and you have at your disposal a great variety of ways with which to work for their eternal destruction. I, myself, spent a considerable number of years in the very line of work to which you now have been assigned. I have earned a favorable standing in Satan's eyes. The record clearly shows an admirable number of souls claimed through my efforts.

Do not misunderstand me, however. The souls to which I am referring were not claimed for Satan by my efforts alone, but rather, it was due to my ability to understand and carry out his intricate and highly effective plans. He is, if you do not already know, the most cunning of all deceivers. Do not ever make the mistake of thinking there are any that surpass him in intelligence or talent when it comes to the destruction of souls.

If you are aspiring to advance in his kingdom, you must

worship him above all, give him all the credit, and always imitate him to the best of your ability. The more you resemble him, the more your work will satisfy him.

As I have already indicated, I have had a great deal of experience in misleading young souls, but I have a particularly good record when it comes to young Catholics. For this reason I have been assigned to oversee your work. I want to make my expectations very clear. I expect results! I do not accept half-hearted efforts, nor do I accept excuses for missed opportunities. Mind you, I will be keeping a strict account and so will, I hope you realize, Satan himself.

Remember, <u>you</u> chose to follow him. You are aspiring to an honorable position in his kingdom. You must prove yourself worthy. You, and those who have been assigned to work with you, must, if you wish to advance, destroy many souls by making them choose our love-empty Kingdom of Darkness over that wonderfully bright, extremely happy Kingdom of Heaven promised by God – our Enemy.

Yours in Darkness,

S corpion

Letter 2

Dear Agent 6,

My correspondence with you will be a series of letters based on my extensive files which, if studied and applied with care and precision, should ensure the success of your efforts to mislead and ultimately destroy many young Catholic souls.

The first and most basic advice I can give you is to keep your own existence a secret. Every good and effective deceiver knows that he can best influence people who think that demons are not real. Disbelief in our existence makes people more vulnerable to certain kinds of deception, so what you want to do is create the idea that we are mythical creatures, figments of the imagination. Make the truth of fallen, rebellious angels turned antagonists appear as an unlikely tale. Let people think of our banishment to Hell as a mere story. They must not grasp its reality. Instead, the truth must be somehow rendered a silly fairy tale, and it must always be made to seem the belief of naive children.

Suggest to young people that growing up necessitates disbelief in our existence, and that belief in such "things" as fallen angels and demonic influences is too unpopular for serious consideration. Ultimately, you want to have as much influence over young people as you can without their ever suspecting it.

Yours in Darkness,

S corpion

Letter 3

Dear Agent 6,

One of the reasons Satan works so desperately to destroy not only Catholic souls, but also the institution of the **Catholic Church**, is that the Catholic priesthood can be traced directly to God's Son during His earthly **Incarnation**. I hope you realize the danger of this fact and understand the reason Satan has worked so tirelessly to obscure this unfortunate truth.

If young Catholic people truly began to understand that their religion has been passed down to them unbroken and divinely authorized, tracing back to Jesus Himself, they would begin to take their religion much too seriously. There would also be an ever-increasing number of them desiring to become **priests** or enter **religious life**. Since Satan has done such a good job of discouraging these desires, he would not be at all pleased to see his work destroyed.

You must do everything you can to hide the truth. Young people must not become convinced that the **Pope** and the **bishops**, as the lawful successors of the **Apostles**, have power from Christ to teach, to sanctify, and to govern the faithful in spiritual matters. Therefore, employ in your effort to obscure the roots of the Catholic Church your best and brightest demons. Choose those who can skillfully create the impression that the Catholic Church has made things up as it went along, or that its teachings and religious practices are out-dated and old-fashioned. This may not be as hard to do as it seems, especially today. Satan has deceived great numbers of people into believing that it is not actually the voice of Christ speaking through those who represent Him in His Church. Many now believe they can make up their own laws. Imagine that!

They are so easy to fool, these young Catholics. They believe they are independent – making their own decisions. They seldom suspect the great numbers of souls we have already claimed through greed, lust, and violence, nor the degree to which we influence their so-called "choices." Take, for example, "their music." What a laugh! We have cultivated many willing performers to advance the marvelous filth and violence they listen to daily. They seldom even question what they are being "taught" through their music. It is exhilarating to see them change their language, dress, and behavior, all the while believing they are in charge. If any of them resists a temptation, distract them. Confuse them. Don't let them think too much. We can't have that!

Above all, block all efforts which may encourage Catholics of any age to trust the Church and its **Magisterium** as a reliable authority on the salvation of souls. Keep them suspicious of the Church's real authority. Otherwise the actual truth may surface, thus encouraging the very kind of faith you are supposed to destroy.

Yours in darkness,

S corpion

Letter 4

Dear Agent 6,

This is just a brief correspondence. I want to be sure you understand why the work of destroying young Catholic souls must begin very early. Satan has a particular hatred for the dastardly Catholic practice of baptizing children soon after their birth. I'm not sure if you have grasped the significance of this horrible practice of infant baptism. By it these souls are quickly ushered into the supernatural life of **grace**, and consequently, they are purified from that **Original Sin** of which Satan was the grand perpetrator.

Satan suffers greatly each time a person is baptized, but especially so in the case of infants. Baptized infant souls are literally wrenched from his grasp soon after birth and freed from the **principal effects of Original Sin**. They are no longer deprived of our Enemy's **sanctifying grace**. Precisely because these Catholic children are so quickly made into children of God and heirs of our Enemy's kingdom, you must begin to draw them away from God's influence as early as possible. Of course, we want to keep them from realizing what gracious acts of generosity infant baptisms are. It would not please Satan if those to

whom you have been assigned began to understand and appreciate the mercy and love God pours into their souls through this
sacrament.

Yours in darkness,

S corpion

Letter 5

Dear Agent 6,

As I stated in my last correspondence, the work of destroying Catholic souls must begin at a very early age. Fortunately for you a great deal of groundwork has already been laid. You and your assistants need only continue the momentum of the plan which Satan has so efficiently set into motion.

I am assuming, of course, you have been well instructed in God's **commandments**. At least it has always been Satan's policy that all of his demons understand thoroughly and in every detail God's laws. Satan believes that a thorough understanding of these laws is necessary before we can entice people to act in ways which contradict them. If all Christians had as thorough an understanding of God's laws as we do, they would be much harder to deceive and, consequently, to entice into sinful behavior.

I guarantee that you will obtain some of the greatest satisfaction of your career when you learn how to entice people to break God's laws. If they have first struggled and resisted a bit, the victory will be even sweeter. And, if you can get them to repress feelings of remorse or guilt afterward, your triumph will be complete. Satan loves this modern attitude of "I had to do what I had to do!" It is to your advantage, therefore, to keep them thinking that their sins are justified by circumstances. Also, Satan is extremely gratified that people are less desirous of performing even small acts of **penance** to atone for their offenses. In these days many no longer believe that acts of self-denial are either necessary or pleasing to God. This is very good and you will gain Satan's approval if you continue to reinforce this trend.

Another very good strategy is to encourage young people to think they somehow greatly honor God if they can at least manage to be a decent person overall, even if they are not necessarily "religious." Also, instill the idea that God's laws are impossibly difficult and very unrealistic. If they are kept in the dark regarding the graces God lavishes on those who sincerely strive to keep His laws and are encouraged to think only of the difficulty involved, they can often be persuaded to think that striving to obey God's laws is a waste of time. Their Guardian Angels will work against all of this, of course, and they will always encourage their charges to truly love and to obey God's laws, but despite the work of the faithful angels, we must persevere in our destructive work.

Whatever else you do, try never to let them grasp the principle of striving, out of love, to keep God's laws. Once a human soul begins to see that God's laws were not given as a yoke, but as a precious gift, or once he or she understands that keeping His laws is a way of showing love for God, the chances of claiming that soul for Satan are seriously reduced.

Always steer young people away from John's Gospel, and if any religion teacher ever assigns John 14:21 ("He who obeys the commandments he has from Me is the man who loves Me . . . ") as material for meditation or prayer, distract them as much as possible.

Yours in darkness,

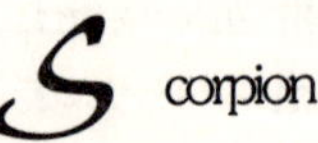

S corpion

Letter 6

Dear Agent 6,

A willful, disobedient, and self-indulgent spirit is what you ultimately want to produce. The first place to start is in the homes and schools. The young people in your charge must not be permitted to take God's commandment "Honor thy father and thy mother" seriously. God is offended by disrespect, unkindness, and disobedience to parents and **lawful superiors**. It is especially painful for Him to watch those who are supposed to belong to Him offend or insult their parents, to whom, after Him, they are indebted for their very lives. See to it, then, that you encourage children and teenagers to show disrespect and unkindness to their parents (and for that matter, also to their teachers) by talking back to them and refusing their correction – or ignoring it. (That works just as well.)

Encourage young people to cause their parents great sorrow through their behavior and attitude, both at home and in school. Often you can cause young people to inflict serious pain upon their parents by encouraging them to develop friendships with people who are a bad influence on them or by inspiring in them the desire for activities and amusements which are dangerous, harmful, or **immoral**. Parents are also hurt when their children display a distaste for things "religious" such as attending Mass, receiving the sacraments, and being attentive to their religious instruction. This latter tactic is extremely torturous to parents who are themselves **devout**. As those assigned to the destruction of adult Catholic souls know, if you cannot get to the parents directly (They are probably too intimate with our Enemy.), you can get to them through their children. I'm telling you, Agent 6, you will squirm with delight when you see the suffering you can cause to these sickeningly devout parents when one of their precious darlings strays. Work hard!

Yours in darkness,

S corpion

Letter 7

Dear Agent 6,

Encourage young people to be disloyal to God and to the Church. Use negative "peer pressure" to help in this effort. Young people must be convinced that giving honor and respect to God, keeping His laws, and behaving reverently will make them unpopular. Suggest to them that these behaviors, are only for "nerds." Satan has worked hard to establish a **stereotype** about intelligent, decent, hardworking kids. His efforts have not been in vain. He has succeeded in causing other young people to regard these decent kids as naive jerks. It works! Use it!

Also, let them feel the sting of social pressure or rejection as early as possible. If they experience rejection or ridicule because they refuse to dishonor God in some way, quickly use it to your advantage. Suggest to them that they are making a sacrifice that is unnecessary, one which even borders on being ridiculous.

If they happen to hear that Jesus warned His followers of persecution, or that He plans to repay them for any and all persecution they may have to endure for His sake, immediately insinuate that His statement is an exaggeration at best. Make them think that He was really only referring to "big" persecutions, like physical torture or death. Hide His true intent. Never let it be known that He means to repay them for every persecution, every suffering, even the everyday inconveniences they may have to patiently endure for His sake. If they fail to understand His real intent, they will also fail to apply His teachings about it on an everyday basis.

If possible, we want them to miss His point entirely. For example, instead of practicing prudence, a virtue highly favored by God which disposes people to reflect on their behavior, to look at things calmly, to judge them rightly, to foresee difficulties, and to take the proper precautions, encourage **impulsiveness** and **self-indulgence**. Keep them focused on how they feel and what they want, not necessarily on the right course of action. Suggest to them that God is actually their harsh judge, and that He demands too much of them. Suggest that He only wants to deprive them of enjoyment and satisfaction.

Let them think that "love" means getting everything they want, however and whenever they want it, and that a God who does not readily indulge whims and desires is not really a God of love. Keep them thinking of happiness in terms of getting what they want or having things go their own way.

You will also do well if you can get them looking for fun and excitement in everything. Let them believe that if something is not "fun," it is "BORING," and therefore, less valuable. You can often discourage attendance at Mass by encouraging young people to dislike it because they think it is "BORING!" If you can get them thinking in terms of boredom, you may be able to keep them thinking that this is a legitimate excuse for not attending Mass, even though it obviously is not. If you are very clever, you might get the parents to go along with this type of thinking. The more **dissension** within the family you can create, especially over such important religious issues as the Mass, the easier it gets to keep them <u>all</u> out of Church. THE LONGER THE BETTER!

Yours in darkness,

S corpion

Letter 8

Dear Agent 6,

I want to discuss an especially crucial aspect of the Catholic Faith with you – the **Eucharist**. I also want to give you some advice on how to undermine it, and undermine it you must! You must be clear on certain points. Once you understand these points, then you can set about confusing these very same points in the minds of young Catholics.

First, the Holy Eucharist is a sacrament and a sacrifice. In the Holy Eucharist under the appearance of bread and wine, the Lord Jesus Christ, our Enemy, is contained, offered, and received. Satan knows that this is the truth, terrible though it is. We demons know that it is the truth. We do not want young Catholics to know it, however. What I mean here is that we do not want them to actually believe it. They can know about it; they can talk about it; they can even give the right answers on tests; but our influence upon them will be greatly reduced if they ever truly believe it. Therefore, work extra hard to discourage belief in the Church's **doctrine** of the Real Presence of Jesus in the Eucharist.

Second, Christ used very clear and explicit words when He

gave the Sacrament of the Eucharist to the Apostles. He did not say, "This is a *symbol* of My Body," or "This *represents* My Body," but "This *Is* My Body." You want, however, to create and maintain ongoing doubt about what He actually said and what He actually meant because, if young Catholics really do as the Church teaches, and on faith they take Christ at His word, they will begin to really believe that it truly is His Body and His Blood. God will give them the grace to do so. Do not let them get that far. Keep them operating on a very superficial level only, and keep suggesting to them that the reception of Holy Communion is only a symbolic gesture – a meal, and nothing more.

Isn't it ironic, Agent 6, that if communicants actually understood the real value of Christ's Eucharistic gift to them they would not dare to approach this sacrament except on their knees? They would die of amazement and gratitude if they could see it and understand it as we do. Fortunately for us, though, while Christ's hidden presence is very real, people usually see only the wafers and the wine. The real threat to us comes when they take that leap of faith and believe what they do not actually see. I am warning you that God's intention for all who receive Him with simple faith is to reward them generously, and He intends to do it in ways that will make all of us demons sick with grief for all eternity. This is why Satan works so hard to undermine faith in this sacrament.

As a general rule it is wise to keep young people from reading John's Gospel, especially John 6:51: "I myself am the living bread come down from heaven. If anyone eat of this bread he shall live forever; and the bread that I give is my flesh for the life of the world." Also try to steer them away from John 6:54: "He who feeds on my flesh and drinks my blood has life eternal and I will raise him up on the last day." If these devastatingly true verses reach their ears, immediately counter them with thoughts of how impossible and ridiculous it all is. Make them forget the excruciatingly painful truth of God's omnipotence – that He can do all things by His almighty power. Make them think that certain things are impossible even to God, especially things like turning bread and wine into His Body and Blood.

I will have more to say on this subject in subsequent letters.

Yours in darkness,

S corpion

Letter 9

Dear Agent 6,

You do realize, don't you, that a soul is greatly benefited and is actually drawn closer to the very life of Christ with each Holy Communion? As disturbing as these facts are, we must face up to the truth. When a soul receives the Sacrament of the Eucharist worthily, there is an increase of that sanctifying grace which our Enemy is so fond of giving. There is also an increase in grace for the practice of all the **virtues**. (I personally think He gives too many graces for so little an effort on their part. Don't you agree, Agent 6?)

If you think I am exaggerating here, just observe carefully the heart of a fervent communicant. Watch how closely the communicant's heart becomes united with the heart of Christ. Notice the divine sweetness our Enemy pours into that soul, and notice, too, the increase of love for God and neighbor. I'm telling you, Agent 6, to a soul in the **state of grace**, this Eucharistic sacrament is not only a further purifier, it is also a pledge of eternal life.

I want you to know why I have chosen to focus on this sacrament ahead of some of the others. Souls receive grace through each of the sacraments, and this is, of course, dreadful to us. But in the Eucharist, they receive the very Author of grace, God Himself. Do not despair, however, because it is not as hopeless a situation as it may appear. Let me explain. First, while we know that all of these generous gifts of grace are procured for the soul in a supernatural, but very real, way through Holy Communion, very few communicants ever actually feel the effects of these graces. You see, much to our advantage, God wants them to believe through faith first. I warn you again, however, that if that dreaded leap of faith is actually undertaken, if the person says, "I choose to believe whether or not I can see or feel anything supernatural; I choose to take God and His Church at their word," you will shudder with disgust at the result.

Mark carefully what I say here. When a person really and truly believes the truth about the Eucharist, that person will amend his or her life and strive to live so conformed to the will of God that nothing will stand between them. The idea is that having received the Eucharist, he or she must now become the body of Christ. He or she must become His hands, hands that care for the sick, the old, and the infirm. That person must become His feet, feet that walk with and comfort the lonely. He or she must become His eyes, eyes that look with compassion on the hurt and the lost. The communicant must also become His voice, a voice willing to speak the truth with power and conviction. What you don't want, Agent 6, is to have that person who is "breaking bread" in the name of Jesus know that he or she is celebrating the brotherhood and sisterhood that binds him or her with the community of Christ. Should that person actually grasp the true sense of Eucharistic community, God may begin to make His actual presence sensibly known to the soul. Should a soul in your charge ever come to this point, should one ever begin to know in the depths of his or her being the actual and real sweet-

ness of God's love, which is eternal life itself, Satan will be out-
raged against you.

You must learn this lesson early. If a communicant's heart
is touched, even once, in a sensible and conscious way by Christ's
own life of love, that person will know evermore that God _is_
real. His presence _is_ real. His love _is_ real. Eternity _is_ real. Heaven
_is_ real! Do not let anyone ever get to the point where they "know"
this is all real. Keep them in the state where they waver back
and forth between, "It's real; it's not real. It's true; it's not true."
In the end we'll have a better chance of claiming them.

Yours in darkness,

S corpion

Letter 10

Dear Agent 6,

We will now consider the aspect of "worthy" communions. You know, of course, what the Church teaches: To receive Holy Communion worthily it is necessary to be free from **mortal sin**, to have a right intention, and to obey the **Church's laws** on the fast before Holy Communion. In each of these prerequisites there is adequate room for misleading souls.

First of all, it should be comforting to know that most of those with whom you are dealing are so inadequately educated, not only about God's commandments, but also about what constitutes sins against them, that it is easy to encourage them to commit sins. There is, however, a specific sin of **sacrilege** which I want to explain to you. This particular sin of sacrilege is committed when a person receives Holy Communion even though he or she is not in a state of grace.

Because people today are generally less informed of the true nature of sin, their consciences are weak. People with a weak **conscience** tend to think that their soul is in a state of grace, even when it is not. If these people are also encouraged to doubt the Church's doctrine on the Real Presence of Jesus in the Eucharist, they can usually be persuaded to believe that it doesn't really matter whether they are in a state of grace or not. However, for those whose conscience is still sharp enough to cause them to suspect that they are not in a state of grace, you can suggest that Holy Communion is only a symbolic gesture anyway. If they think Communion is only symbolic and not the actual Body and Blood of Christ, they will be more apt to believe that being in the state of grace is also only a symbolic requirement and not necessarily a binding one. This tactic has been working very well for about two decades. There is ample reason to expect it to continue working. At any rate, it's well worth the effort!

Pride and peer pressure can also be used to lead your charges into the sin of sacrilegious Communion. Suppose a communicant doubts his or her state of worthiness due to serious sin. Suggest to that person that in this case it would probably be better to go to Communion anyway rather than to have one's friends, associates, or in the case of a young person, one's parents, think he or she has sinned seriously. Also, it often helps to suggest that under these particular circumstances, (especially if the circumstances concern one's parents) the Lord will understand. Even though this is outrageously false, young people often believe it. Since receiving Communion sacrilegiously is a grave sin, it is one which pleases Satan very much. You should encourage it at every turn.

There are other excellent tactics to use, however. In addition to a soul free from mortal sin, Christ wants to find dispositions of humility and faith in those who receive Him. Actually, no one is truly worthy of the Eucharistic gift, but you can make them think that they are. While venial sins do not destroy the life of grace in a soul, and while they do not prevent a person from receiving Holy Communion, a person should always approach the sacrament with a sincere and contrite heart – which means, Agent 6, that they should be sorry for even their minor offenses and should make an effort to apologize to God. A sincere *Act of Contrition* offered to God before receiving Communion is pleasing to Him, so discourage this. Instead, promote a very casual attitude toward receiving Holy Communion and encourage people to think of receiving it as a personal right instead of as a privileged gift. An attitude of pride will discourage the **humility** Christ desires in those with whom He humbly shares Himself.

The fasting requirements for Holy Communion are to refrain from food and drink, except water, for one hour prior to receiving the Eucharist. (Medicine can be taken at any time.) While these requirements are minimal, they are binding. It is helpful to encourage people to think of the fast as optional, as a helpful suggestion, but as one which can be put aside if it causes even the slightest inconvenience. People can usually provide rational excuses for not meeting the fasting requirements, and you can help them along a little by suggesting to them that they are just using the common sense God gave them. (They are supposed to adjust the circumstances of their lives to fit the fasting requirements and not the other way around. You would think it would be obvious!)

Have you begun to wonder how these Catholic people can be so gullible? It is because Satan has allocated many legions of tempters to work especially on them. As I mentioned previously, the Catholic Church is guarding the total deposit of Christian truth which has been given to Her by Jesus Himself. Through the Catholic Church the actual presence of Christ is preserved in the Eucharist. This is why Satan continually attacks Catholics and their truth-bearing Church from all angles.

If he can, Satan will destroy the Catholic Church entirely,

and just think of the immense pleasure and satisfaction you will gain knowing that you played such an important part in its destruction. For your information, however, he commands us to ignore the truth that Jesus stated during His earthly Incarnation, namely that He will remain with His Church until the end of time, and that the gates of Hell shall not prevail against it. Do not give this statement too much thought or you may become discouraged unnecessarily.

Yours in darkness,

S corpion

Letter 11

Dear Agent 6,

You understand by now that Christ, our Enemy, does actually and really give His own Body and Blood in the Holy Eucharist, but do you know why He does this? Again, if you are going to effectively undermine this dreaded gift, you must know exactly what aspects of it to attack.

For the record, Christ gives His own Body and Blood in the Holy Eucharist to be offered as a sacrifice commemorating and renewing for all time the sacrifice of the cross. He also desires to be received by the faithful in Holy Communion, to remain ever on their altars as the proof of His love for them, and to be worshipped by them.

God really does love these people of His, Agent 6. He loves every member of the human race so very much that He devised this means of Holy Communion so He could – if they choose to cooperate with Him – be their intimate companion in every age and in every part of the world. Whatever else you do, always work to obscure the immense power and goodness of the Eucharist. We especially do not want young people to know that Christ is present in this sacrament to be the friend and brother of their souls or the comfort, strength, and joy of their lives.

Every hour, somewhere in the world, the Holy Sacrifice of the Mass is offered, and Jesus becomes Eucharistically present on the altar. Conceal, as well as you can, this truth about the Mass. You must circulate the mistaken idea that attending any church's service where the Word of God is preached is as pleasing to God as is the Holy Sacrifice of the Mass.

The Mass is the sacrifice of the **New Covenant** in which Christ, through the ministry of the priest, offers Himself to God in an unbloody manner under the appearances of bread and wine. We want you to conceal this fact as well. Even though young people attend Sunday Mass faithfully, we do not want it to be clear to them why they are really there, or that what they have been told is supposed to happen during the Mass, really does happen. Remember, God is waiting for an act of faith on their part. He is waiting for that singular decision – to believe what they can not actually see. You do not want such faith to develop, though. Should real faith develop in those whose faith you are charged to destroy, Satan's wrath will be unleashed against you.

There is still more to consider. The Church teaches that the first sentiment of the hearts of the faithful toward their Lord in the Blessed Sacrament should be one of profound adoration, reverence, gratitude, and respect since He is God. Encourage, instead, indifference, casualness, ingratitude, and a lack of reverence.

The second sentiment toward the Blessed Sacrament which the Church advances is ardent love based on the fact that Jesus remains on their altars out of love for them. Encourage a feeling of vague sentimentality, but not one of real love and appreciation.

Thirdly, if the Church had its way, people of all ages would be proving their love for Jesus in the Holy Eucharist by participating in Mass and receiving Holy Communion as often as possible, by attending **Benediction**, by making visits to the Blessed Sacrament, by making acts of desire to receive **Spiritual Communion**, by spending an hour in adoration when the Blessed Sacrament is exposed, and by many other devotions. Encourage them to think that such devotions are unnecessary in these modern times. Remember, keep genuine love out of the picture as much as possible.

Yours in darkness,

S corpion

Letter 12

Dear Agent 6,

I can certainly see that you are benefiting by my instruction. I am particularly pleased to observe a sharp increase in the number of sacrilegious Communions your charges are receiving. This is very good! This is my final instruction to you regarding the Eucharist. It has to do with certain actions taken by our Enemy to provide true and lasting proof of His miraculous presence in this sacrament. I will provide for you one example of what I mean and will leave it to you to discover for yourself subsequent actions of this nature. You must go to great lengths to cover up all such evidences.

I have chosen to explain the Eucharistic Miracle of Lanciano, Italy because it has contained for over twelve centuries the first and greatest Eucharistic Miracle of the Catholic Church. It took place in the 8th Century A.D. in a little church named St. Legontian. A particular Basilian monk, one our agent had been working on for some time, was very doubtful regarding the Real Presence in the Eucharist.

During Mass, after the **Consecration**, the host was transformed into live Flesh and the wine was transformed into live

Blood. The blood coagulated into five globules. These globules of blood were irregular and differed in shape and size. Since 1713, the Flesh has been reserved in a silver **ostensorium**. The Blood is enclosed in a rich and very old cup made of Rock-crystal.

Various ecclesiastical investigations have been conducted. The most outstanding, however, and the most devastating for us, was the scientific investigation conducted in 1970. The Church employed two prominent scientists: Odoardo Linoli, an Eminent Professor in Anatomy and Pathological Histology and in Chemistry and Clinical Microscopy, and professor Ruggero Bertelli of the University of Siena who acted as his assistant.

Agent 6, there is no question about the scientific precision with which the analyses were conducted. They were documented with a series of microscopic photographs which were rendered a matter of public domain by the esteemed Professor Linoli himself in a conference held on March 4, 1971.

With scientific evidence as proof, the following conclusions were given:

- The Flesh is human Flesh. The Blood is human Blood.
- The Flesh consists of the muscular tissue of the heart (myocardium).
- The Flesh and the Blood have the same blood type (AB).
- In the Blood there were found proteins in the same normal proportions (percentage wise) as are found in the sero-proteic make-up of fresh normal blood.
- In the Blood there were also found these minerals: chloride, phosphorus, magnesium, potassium, sodium, and calcium.
- The preservation of the Flesh and of the Blood, which were left in their natural state for twelve centuries with-

out any chemical preservatives and which were exposed to atmospheric and biological agents, is an extraordinary phenomenon.

It is obvious, is it not, why events of this nature must remain hidden? Just think, Agent 6, of what would happen if too many young Catholics became aware of the many phenomenal miracles entrusted to the Church. Do you want them really believing that they do truly receive the Body and Blood of Christ? Absolutely not! Then you must become very astute at covering up the miraculous proofs which our Enemy has given them.

Yours in darkness,

S corpion

Letter 13

Dear Agent 6,

I understood that when you took your new position you had at least some expertise and skill in distracting souls. My observations indicate that you are not as skilled in creating distractions as I first assumed. So let me share with you some of the ways and reasons for causing distractions, especially during Mass, particularly during the Consecration and at Communion time.

You may have noticed that I often instruct you in what the Church teaches so you know what specific things to discourage. In keeping with this, then, let me state that the proper way for the faithful to assist at Mass is with reverence, attention, and devotion. You will recall that in the Holy Mass, Jesus Christ offers to God the Father, through the ministry of the priest, the gift of His Body and Blood, the same gift once presented on Calvary. The congregation's part in the Holy Mass is to join with Christ in offering Himself to God the Father and to receive His Body and Blood in Holy Communion.

Because the Mass is the unbloody renewal of the passion and death of Jesus Christ, whenever it is celebrated, it causes a terrible anguish to Satan and to all of his followers. Since Masses are offered continuously throughout the world, you can imagine the hatred Satan has for this painful celebration. He commands us to put forth a valiant effort to distract and annoy all who assist in this dreadful reenactment of Calvary.

During the Mass the faithful are supposed to assist devoutly by following the priest step by step, prayer by prayer, and by answering the responses, meditating on the Word, and singing the hymns. Distract them by introducing other matters for their consideration. Get them to watch and observe other people, to pay attention to their clothing or hairstyles or jewelry. Entice them to think about what they will do later in the day, or what they did the day before. Suggest to them ideas contrary to what is happening during the Mass, so that whole segments of the Mass can be enacted while their minds and hearts are somewhere else entirely. If they try, with the aid of their Guardian Angel, to bring their thoughts back to the Mass and strive for **recollection**, come at them again with some petty anxiety or problem to mull over, especially at the time of the Consecration.

The Church teaches that it is proper before Communion for a person to spend some time thinking of Jesus and ardently desiring to receive Him. This is an excellent time to suggest to them other matters for consideration, anything to draw their hearts and minds away from thoughts of Jesus.

After Communion is also a good time to work hard at causing distractions. While they should be spending time adoring the Lord, thanking Him, renewing promises of love and obedience to Him, and asking Him for blessings for themselves and others, direct their attention to trivial, everyday matters. You can even capitalize on the hunger they may naturally feel due to the Eucharistic fast by stimulating thoughts about what they will eat for breakfast or lunch that day.

You do see the point of this "distraction" business, don't

you? Those who learn to ply their craft well are numbered among Satan's most favored deceivers.

Yours in darkness,

S corpion

Letter 14

Dear Agent 6,

It seems your skill in causing "distractions" has improved considerably. I hope you prove to be even more detrimental to souls in this next area, a very crucial one – the Sacrament of Reconciliation. How deeply Satan hates the practice of confession! If you become very skilled in keeping people from the habit of regular confession, there is no limit to how far you can advance.

For the record, the Church teaches that during His life on earth, Christ forgave sinners by His own authority. Before ascending into Heaven, as a means of providing for the spiritual needs of His followers, He **conferred** the power of forgiving sins on His Apostles and their successors. No man, by his own power and authority, could possibly forgive sins. Only God can do that because sin is an offense against Him.

Priests do not remit sin of their own authority, Agent 6, but by the authority entrusted to them by God. This is an easy teaching to confuse, and such confusion can be used to our advantage, especially if instruction on this point remains sketchy, incomplete, or unclear. Poorly instructed people are more apt to doubt the necessity of confessing sins to a priest. If they do not believe it is necessary to confess sins to a priest, you can usually keep them out of the confessional for long periods of time. This is what Satan wants.

Another point I want to make clear to you is that the Church's priests are not givers of grace. The Church has never taught that they are, for that would imply divine power. They are, however, ministers of dispensing God's grace. The priest has the power from Jesus Christ to forgive sins and dispense God's grace. Check for yourself. Read John 20:22-23: "Then He breathed on them and said: 'Receive the Holy Spirit. If you forgive men's sins, they are forgiven them; if you hold them bound, they are held bound.'"

As I mentioned earlier, you want young people to be somewhat confused and unclear about confession. Here are some of the false ideas we have been advancing for years, and in many cases these ideas have had the effect we want. First, we have suggested that confession is an invention of the **clergy** and has no divine sanction. Although this is not true, we have created this impression by using influences which originate from outside of the Church. Second, we have encouraged people to think it is just as effective to confess sins directly to God, rather than through a priest in the confessional. Third, we have advanced the idea that priests, after all, are just men. We have quite successfully played down the fact that the Sacrament of **Holy Orders** imprints on the soul of the priest a **character**, lasting forever, which is a special sharing in the priesthood of Christ, and which gives the priest special supernatural powers. Chief among the supernatural powers is the power to change bread and wine into the Body and Blood of Christ in the holy Sacrifice of the Mass as well as the power to forgive sins in the Sacrament of Reconciliation. If young people continue to accept false ideas instead of true ones, we predict that they will continue to feel little need for the Sacrament of Reconciliation.

You may also want to tempt young people through pride by inflating their feelings of embarrassment and by encouraging reluctance to confess their sins to a priest. This can be accomplished, again, by concealing the true role of the priest in confession. You realize, don't you, that the priest actually "stands in" for Jesus in this sacrament? By the priest's actual and personal presence the **penitent** receives the benefit of a two-way vocal dialogue through which specific guidance can be given if needed. The penitent is also assured of God's forgiveness because God's **absolution** and His blessing are both bestowed verbally through the instrumentality of the priest. Blind young people to the extremely beneficial and merciful aspects of this sacramental gift of reconciliation, and you will have accomplished much for Satan's cause. Just think of the peace they will miss and the grace they will forfeit if they give up the practice of confession!

Let me clarify several more points. First, when people receive the Sacrament of Reconciliation worthily, it restores or increases sanctifying grace in their souls. Satan commands us to conspire against gifts of grace. Second, this sacrament also remits eternal punishment. Satan receives immense satisfaction when he claims a soul eternally. You do not want to disappoint him do you? Third, through this sacrament souls can reduce their time of purification in **Purgatory**. Those who make regular, sincere, worthy confession a life-time habit are an absolute threat to Satan! And the reasons why this sacrament is so threatening do not stop with those I've already listed. The humility required in confessing one's sins confounds Satan's pride. This sacrament also blunts the force of temptation, disposes people to pray better, helps them to break bad habits, gives strength to the will, and sharpens the conscience to discern sinful behavior. The Sacrament of Reconciliation also helps them grow in holiness, thus improving their relationship with God. You can see why the conspiracy against the Sacrament of Reconciliation must continue with increased effort.

In addition, the Sacrament of Reconciliation, when worthily received, helps one to avoid sin in the future because it weakens the power of temptation. The danger of this should be obvious. And finally, this hateful sacrament restores the merits of good works if they were formerly lost by serious sin. Satan wants people to die in the state of serious sin. That way they are deprived of the merits of their good works. This weighs the scale heavily in our favor and pleases Satan very much.

Yours in darkness,

S corpion

Letter 15

Dear Agent 6,

In speaking of the Sacrament of Reconciliation, I mentioned that it must be received worthily. There are five conditions necessary for a worthy confession and each can be used to our advantage.

The first condition necessitates the examination of one's conscience. In an examination of one's conscience one calls to mind the sins committed since the last worthy confession. You can render an examination of conscience less effective either by encouraging carelessness or by encouraging excessive anxiety.

An **examination of conscience** done in haste may leave certain sins unconfessed due to forgetfulness, so you want to discourage penitents from taking the time to consider each of the commandments. Whenever a person does take the time to check themselves against what each commandment teaches (regarding what to do or to avoid), the examination of conscience is apt to be thorough. Satan does not want this. On the other hand, if you can manage to incite excessive anxiety during an examination of conscience, the penitent may tend to omit the confession of certain sins out of pride, embarrassment, or fear.

Satan highly approves of this.

Not only should an examination of conscience call to mind the commandments of God, but it should also lead one to ask if he or she is faithfully fulfilling the particular duties of one's state in life. I will wager, Agent 6, that these days you would be hard pressed to find many who even know what the words "duties of one's state in life" mean. This ignorance is a legacy of which you should be proud!

There are, for example, certain Christian duties required of those who are in religious orders. There are other Christian duties required of those who have undertaken the vocation of marriage. For those to whom you have been assigned, there are also certain Christian duties.

As members of a family young people are to respect and obey their parents and to contribute to the welfare of the family. They do this by a willingness to submit to the rules and guidelines parents set, by the faithful fulfillment of designated chores and responsibilities, and by setting a good example for younger brothers and sisters.

As students they are required to respect and obey their teachers, to use well the mental capacity with which God has endowed them, to achieve and learn with honesty and integrity, and to behave responsibly by meeting the demands of learning.

As members of the Church their Christian duty calls them to lovingly and willingly respect and comply with the commandments of God and the Precepts of the Church, to set a good example for others to follow, to be faithful witnesses for Christ in thought, word, and deed, and to participate fully in the Church community and in the worship of God. By blocking the knowledge of the duties of their state in life, you can get young people to avoid the examination of whole segments of their lives.

You want young people to be oblivious to the idea of "Christian duty." Instead, encourage them to think that a relationship with God is primarily based on what God can do for them, not on what they can do for God. You also want to discourage them from confessing sins of omission. Sins of omission are the ways they have failed to fulfill their Christian duties, especially of their particular state in life. Ignorance of sin makes it easier, not only to tempt people to sin in the first place, but also to render their confessions less effective since they will tend to be less aware of their true offenses.

Yours in darkness,

S corpion

Letter 16

Dear Agent 6,

To receive the Sacrament of Reconciliation worthily also necessitates a second condition – contrition or sincere sorrow for sin. Sorrow for sin is so essential to this sacrament that God, although omnipotent, cannot forgive the sins of one who is not **repentant**.

You are not above telling a very destructive lie, are you, Agent 6? Frankly, I hope you are an excellent liar because you will then resemble Satan all the more. He was a liar from the beginning. Not only must you be a very good liar, you must also be a very convincing one. The real power behind any lie comes from the ability to convince people that what is not true is actually true. In the matter of contrition or sorrow for sin, you will find great potential for deceiving people. It is done by promoting Satan's most fundamental lie.

This fundamental lie of which I speak has several parts. The first part of the lie goes like this: *God is not seriously offended by sin because He is too big, too kind, too merciful, too forgiving, and too loving.* You want them to think He is a "wimp," too "soft" to actually reject them. In other words, you want them to believe that in the end, no matter what a person has done or how he or she has lived, God will grant everyone, even the unrepentant, eternal life and happiness because He is such a loving and merciful God. (Of course, they do not understand that their greatest punishment lies in being separated from Him forever, nor that Satan's greatest delight is in depriving them of eternal happiness.)

The second part of the lie follows from the first: *Since God is not really as offended by sin as much as the priests, religion teachers, and parents make it seem that He is, then sin is not that big of a deal.* Why would they feel sorry for something which is not offensive?

You not only want them to believe that God is not greatly offended by sin, you also want them to believe that *self-fulfillment justifies sinful behavior*, so that is the third part of the lie. In other words, they must really believe that if it takes sinful behavior to feel satisfied and fulfilled in life, then God will understand the necessity of sinful behavior. You also want to promote the belief that if sinful behavior is, in their eyes, necessary for reaching their full potential in life, or for getting what they want, then their sinful ways are justified. The end justifies the means – <u>truly a classic deception!</u>

Yours in darkness,

S corpion

Letter 17

Dear Agent 6,

Any of the parts of the great fundamental lie will prevent true contrition or sincere sorrow for sins, and this is good. I also want to explain how to lead your charges into another error – the sin of presumption.

A person sins by presumption when he or she knowingly sins against God while presuming that it is all right to do so since he or she will soon confess the sin. In this error one's thought process is typically, "I know I should not do this because it is wrong, but I'll go ahead and do it anyway since I can go to confession and have it forgiven." In effect, the person is taking advantage of God's merciful nature and is also misusing the Sacrament of Reconciliation.

Another form of presumption occurs when a person knowingly places himself or herself in the "near occasion of sin." Here is an example. A person suspects that by going to a certain place or event, for example, to a party or to a particular movie, or that by keeping the company of certain people who are a bad influence on him or her, he or she is very likely to fall into sinful behavior. Yet, that person goes to that place or event or socializes with those people of bad influence anyway. That person is "tempting" God. It is like saying to Him, "I am going to do this even though I am likely to offend You in the process. You must give me the grace to avoid sin even though I am willing to place myself very near to an occasion of committing it."

This matter of "presumption" is a subtle, but effective way of leading people into offensive, sinful behavior. Once you lead them into the pattern of presuming on God's mercy in small things, you can usually lead them into presuming on God's mercy in more serious matters as well. It becomes easier and easier for a person to knowingly offend God, to disobey parents, to entertain evil thoughts, to use offensive language, to look at indecent pictures, to listen to suggestive music or jokes, to lie, to cheat, to steal, to engage in premarital sex, to live together before marriage, or to fail to do one's duty by presuming ahead of time on God's mercy.

Presumption is wrong, of course, and the Church prohibits this attitude. Nevertheless, a good deceiver knows how to lead people into the sin of presumption anyway.

Yours in darkness,

S corpion

Letter 18

Dear Agent 6,

So far I have covered several ways to undermine the first two conditions for a worthy confession: examination of conscience and sincere contrition. Before I cover the other three conditions, I want to talk about a sin which is particularly easy to encourage. It is the sin of "detraction." Detraction occurs when one reveals unnecessarily another's faults, shortcomings, weaknesses, or sins and, as a consequence, diminishes that person's reputation. Detraction is a sin against God's eighth commandment, "Thou shalt not bear false witness against thy neighbor." By this commandment the faithful are required to speak the truth in all things, but especially in what concerns the good reputation and honor of others.

You see, Agent 6, to God a good reputation is a most precious possession. God feels so strongly about this matter of a good reputation that He has protected this right through His eighth commandment. He obliges respect for others by not making known their faults when one has no right to do so and by not making false accusations against others. It is the "duty" of Christians to think well and to speak well of others. Only God can penetrate to the interior of a person's conscience and scrutinize his or her intentions. He alone can judge with truth and justice.

A person injures another by backbiting, by malicious gossip, by revealing a secret one has been asked to keep, and especially, by **calumniating** or slandering another, that is by falsely charging another with defects or sins. Backbiting, gossiping, not keeping a secret, and lying about a person are sins which are fairly easy to recognize, but the sin of "detraction" is a little more subtle, and it is this subtlety which makes it an easy sin to encourage. Even though what one reveals about the other person is "true," damaging another's reputation is not approved of by God. He wants His people to go out of their way to protect the good name and reputation of their fellowman.

You should not only encourage the sin of detraction, you should also discourage any clarity as to why God considers detraction sinful. You should also discourage young people from confessing sins of detraction. Of course, they will be less likely to confess instances of detraction if they fail to recognize it as sinful in the first place.

Yours in darkness,

S corpion

Letter 19

Dear Agent 6,

Satan is very satisfied with your progress. We can't help but notice that the lines outside the confessionals are shorter. We have also noticed that there are fewer young people in those lines. You are making admirable strides. Keep up the good work!

Now, I'll continue with my instructions on the other three conditions for a worthy confession. The three other conditions necessary for a worthy confession are to have the firm purpose of not sinning again, to confess the sins verbally to a priest, and to be willing to perform the penance the priest gives.

The firm purpose of not sinning again is the sincere resolve not only to avoid sin in the future, but also to avoid, as far as possible, the near occasions of sin. Rather than the knowledge and understanding that they are required to avoid persons, places, or things that may lead to sin, suggest to young people that they are heroes for God when they knowingly place themselves in potentially sinful situations and then struggle to avoid falling into sin. Chances are that if you can get them into the potentially sinful environment or situation in the first place, add a healthy dose of negative peer pressure, and play upon their strong adolescent need for acceptance and approval, you can gain a sweet victory. They do not realize that our success is more or less a sure thing the moment they consciously decide to place themselves near to the occasion of the sin.

Now, as to that condition of having a sincere resolve not to sin again, Satan's great fundamental lie will easily undermine resolutions of that nature. People who do not really believe that God is greatly offended by sin, or that He has a "just" as well as a "merciful" nature, will not see a great need to resolve against sin. Their attitude toward sin will be a very casual one, and once again, the habit of "presumption" will play an important part in this.

If he could, Satan would prevent people from going to confession altogether, but although you may not be able to give him what he wants, at least do not let them get too comfortable with the practice of confessing sins to a priest. The priest will forgive their sins in the name of Christ, advise and encourage them if necessary, help them resolve doubts, and guide their future conduct. Never, under any circumstances, not even to save his life, will a priest reveal the sins that have been confessed to him. This is known as the "Seal of Confession." Are you beginning to understand more clearly why Satan says, "Destroy this hateful practice of confessing sins to a priest!"?

Finally, the condition of performing the penance given by the priest must be considered. For the record, the priest assigns a penance after confession so that the penitent may make some reparation to God for his or her sins, receive help to avoid sin in the future, and to make some satisfaction for the temporal punishment due to sin.

Temporal punishment refers to the reparation one must make for one's sins. If satisfaction for one's sins is not made in this life, it will be made in Purgatory. God requires temporal punishment for sin to satisfy His justice, to teach people the great evil of sin, and to warn them not to sin again. Christ, by His death on the cross, made more than adequate satisfaction to atone for the temporal punishment due to all the sins of mankind. God, however, wants them to perform works of penance themselves in order to receive all the benefits of the satisfaction of Christ.

Ordinarily, the priest gives only a few prayers as penance, but he may sometimes ask a person to perform a good deed. All penances are to be performed with devotion and gratitude to God, so this is an excellent time to apply your best distraction techniques. You want them to perform their penances quickly and with little real devotion, thought, or gratitude to God.

Of course, if they were a bit smarter about all of this, they would make an effort to perform penances voluntarily. In this way they could pay their debt for temporal punishment during their earthly life, and not in Purgatory. They could also offer their penances on behalf of others, especially for those who would not be inclined to do so for themselves, but who are in need of these graces.

Take care to discourage any thoughts of doing voluntary penances, otherwise you will have people praying more often, attending weekday Masses, making acts of self-denial throughout the year (not just during Lent), making sacrifices, performing charitable deeds, and patiently enduring hardships and difficulties. They would help save a great number of souls. Satan would not be pleased. I can guarantee that!

Yours in darkness,

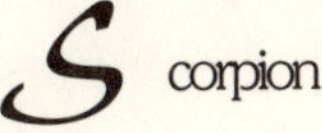 corpion

Letter 20

Dear Agent 6,

There is one more sacrament which is of particular importance to your young charges. I am speaking of the Sacrament of Confirmation.

Through the Sacrament of Confirmation the Holy Spirit comes to souls in a special way, enabling them to profess their Faith as more mature followers of Christ. Confirmation increases sanctifying grace and gives them strength to overcome the dangers and obstacles to salvation. It also imprints a lasting character on the soul and infuses it with a greater abundance of the **gifts of the Holy Spirit**.

You must not only work diligently to discourage the reception of this sacrament, but also to diminish its effects. Consider the following points. First, if you have been successful in tempting young souls in the ways I have already outlined, they should be in a fairly weakened condition spiritually by the time they are preparing for Confirmation. The very weakened ones will shy away from the preparation process, especially if it is a fairly demanding one. It will appear to be too much trouble for something which they now (thanks to our good work) see as having very little value.

Second, by the time young people reach the early teen years they are, for the most part, used to asserting their own will and getting their own way in most things. Fortunately for us, Satan has greatly weakened the role of parents as authority figures in the home. Consequently, if you can encourage young people to moan, groan, and complain about attending religious education classes, or even to outrightly refuse to attend them once they reach high school, many will never be confirmed. Unfortunately for them, they will be deprived of the spiritual grace and strength this sacrament gives. Fortunately for you, however, they will be less able to resist the many temptations with which you and your associates will surround them.

Third, as with each of the other sacraments I have discussed, Confirmation also has certain conditions which are required for proper reception. Candidates for Confirmation must be well instructed in the chief truths and duties of their religion and approach the sacrament in the state of grace. Furthermore, candidates must have as their **sponsors**, baptized and confirmed Catholics.

Rather than thorough instruction, create an appetite for vague, sensational, trendy approaches to preparation for this sacrament. Then encourage the teachers and parents to satisfy these desires. Let them all agree that it is better to at least get young people to the classes, rather than to discourage them by setting high standards and expectations. This is a very popular type of thinking and usually works fairly well.

Fourth, after being confirmed, a Catholic should continue to study his or her religion so that he or she may be able to explain and defend it, but you do not want to promote this. What you want to do is to promote the idea that Confirmation is the end of all necessary training and study in the Faith. By the promotion of this premise, many confirmed Catholics have dropped out of organized religious education programs, feel no need for further reading or study, and some have even discontinued the practice of their Faith. Overall, this will be true for those whose faith foundation and development was very weak. Spiritual weakness makes their eventual destruction so much easier!

Yours in darkness,

S corpion

Letter 21

Dear Agent 6,

Satan has tirelessly worked to replace worship and love of the One True God with worship and love of false gods. Worship of false gods is expressly forbidden by God's first commandment, "I am the Lord thy God; thou shalt have no other gods before Me." Since this was God's first command to the Israelites, it is obvious that His desire not to be replaced in any way by other gods is of primary importance to Him. Satan, therefore, bids us to do whatever we can to entice people of all ages to disobey God's first commandment and put other gods ahead of Him.

The Church teaches explicitly regarding the first commandment. By it the faithful are obliged to believe, love, adore, and serve God alone. They are to believe in God by knowing Him as He has been revealed and by accepting His teachings. They are to love Him by observing His commandments and by behaving charitably toward each other. They are to adore Him by recognizing Him as their supreme Master and by acknowledging their complete dependence upon Him. They are also obliged to give Him proper worship. They are to serve Him through prayer and a Christian life. They owe to God, by His first commandment, exterior as well as interior worship, because their bodies, as well as their souls, belong to Him.

Encourage, then, all types of sins which directly violate this first commandment. Encourage impiety, which is the refusal to offer God the supreme worship He is due. Impiety is seen in the person who does not go to Mass, who disrespects or ignores God, the commandments, the sacraments, the saints, or holy things.

Encourage superstition. Superstition is any practice which gives false worship to God or undue honor to created things. It includes belief in the use of charms and spells, belief in dreams, fortune-telling, seances, astrological signs and horoscopes, unlucky days and numbers, as well as belief in omens such as breaking a mirror, walking under a ladder, or having one's path crossed by a black cat.

The **New Age Movement** has popularized a number of superstitious practices. Satan definitely desires us to encourage such things as **Tarot Cards**, **Ouija boards**, occult board games, occult computer games, **UFOs**, **crystals**, and **channeling of spirit guides**. (These so-called spirit guides are really our agents in disguise, but these **"channels,"** desirous as they are for supernatural experiences, don't believe this.) Also thanks to the New Age Movement, belief in **reincarnation** is very popular. All of these things open one up to Satan's hidden influence in one way or another, so they are all very good things to encourage.

There are two other excellent ways to encourage sins against God's first commandment. One is through heresy. A person sins by heresy when, although a baptized Catholic, he or she refuses to accept one or more of the truths revealed by God and taught by the Catholic Church. With the spread of Satan's increasingly popular philosophy that one can decide for oneself what truths to believe or not to believe, or what one will accept and what one will reject, heresy, even among "good" Catholics is increasing. (For your information, spreading heresy within the Catholic Church is one of Satan's "pet" projects.)

Another sin against the first commandment which is definitely worth advancing is indifferentism. You can encourage the sin of indifferentism by advancing the belief that one religion is as good as another and that all religions are equally true and pleasing to God. Or, you can encourage the belief that each individual is free to accept or reject any or all religions. If possible, you want even those who know that the Catholic Church is the true Church of Jesus Christ to hesitate to accept the Catholic Faith because of the sacrifices that are associated with it. Consider the stricter moral code, confession, the marriage laws, the Church's teaching on artificial contraception, and her firm stand against abortion.

Circulate this convenient theme: "One religion is as good as another." It is a rather popular way of thinking in these modern times, thanks to Satan's powerful propaganda campaign. By the way, be sure you express dutiful support and appreciation for his tremendous success in advancing this belief.

Yours in darkness,

S corpion

Letter 22

Dear Agent 6,

We will now consider the issue of **prayer**. Prayer, undertaken properly and with perseverance, can be a most devastating power against us. Wherever possible, redirect any serious intentions of prayer so that within a given period of time the person either gives up the practice altogether or, at the very least, prays infrequently and only in times of great need.

Many people do not realize that prayer is a high privilege they share with the angels. Yes, it is unnecessarily generous of God to allow these creatures of His to speak with Him in prayer. But, like it or not, wherever prayer is present, God takes noticeable interest. Should prayer become a daily dedicated commitment, there is the added danger that God will begin to engage that soul in a daily rendezvous of love and mercy.

Let me describe the type of prayer that renders our situation desperate. Ten to twenty minutes of the type of committed prayer I am about to explain can be so impressively helpful in producing continual spiritual progress, that you must work against it as if everything depended on destroying this one thing. I'm not exaggerating here. Even ten minutes of devout prayer each day (Of course, longer periods are worse for us!), preferably at the same time of day, in which one of your young charges places himself or herself in the presence of God is detrimental to us. If the person implores God's assistance, adores Him and expresses love and loyalty, thanks God for His favors and graces, requests with a sincere and contrite heart pardon for sins and the remission of punishment, and asks for graces and blessings for self and others an immensity of God's goodness will flow to that soul and will cause you extreme terror.

Through prayer people obtain the grace to resist our temptations, to grow in love for God and in generosity toward others, to persevere in leading a life of faith, and especially, to obtain from God the grace of eternal life. Since prayer is one of the conditions God has laid down for His human creatures to obtain His graces and blessings, you can see the great value in discouraging prayer in all its forms.

All demons must work hard to keep people from seriously committing themselves to prayer, especially the type of prayer which has as its principal motivation the love of God Himself and not just the hope of what God can do for the person at a particular time. When people pray daily and are committed to praying with no regard as to whether their situation at that time is pleasant or difficult, but pray because it is God's pleasure they are seeking and not their own, our influence on them is so greatly reduced that our situation becomes hopeless.

Do you want to please Satan, Agent 6? Then cause those whom he has entrusted to you to avoid prayer and to neglect the great affair of their eternal salvation.

Yours in darkness,

S corpion

Letter 23

Dear Agent 6,

There are other forms of prayer with which you must be familiar. Two, in particular, are especially dangerous. You must assemble your forces and prepare to exert tremendous pressure against both of these forms of prayer.

The first is a form of mental prayer, similar in some respects to the form of devout prayer I described in my last letter. If you observe the following pattern in a person's prayer life, prepare to launch an aggressive counterattack. First, the person places himself or herself in the presence of God and implores His assistance. Next, he or she reads some spiritual book with attention or represents to his or her mind a particular mystery of redemption, certain eternal truths, or (very devastating!) specific scenes from the life and passion of Jesus Christ. Then, the person reflects upon and considers what he or she has read or presented to his or her mind until the affections of the heart are moved and raised up to God.

Now, if the person also adds a practical resolution to correct faults, returns thanks to God for His goodness and mercy, and implores Him to bless the resolution made, you are nearing the end of any real influence upon that soul because that person has now put in your path one of the greatest obstacles to sin – a sincere and committed life of mental prayer.

The second form of prayer against which you must wage an all-out battle (it even causes me pain to name it!) is the **Rosary**. Satan has a very personal hatred for the Rosary because it is so closely associated with Mary, Christ's mother. She is a very powerful heavenly ally for souls, but for us she is an even more powerful adversary. It is true, Agent 6. God has willed this.

Satan commands us to discourage the praying of the Rosary altogether, but that is not always possible. The Mother of God has actually appeared to several elected individuals in a very real and tangible form throughout the centuries since the establishment of her Son's Church. In these appearances she always asks very directly that the faithful pray the Rosary, so it is unlikely that we will be able to get rid of this very powerful form of prayer. However, at least discourage your young people from learning how to pray the Rosary devoutly. Especially keep them from devout meditation upon the mysteries of the Rosary. When prayed correctly, the Rosary becomes a meditation undertaken together with Mary.

Fortunately, Satan has hidden this fact from the great majority of Catholics and has succeeded in promoting the misconception that the Rosary is merely a monotonous, routine form of prayer with little value. Imagine what would happen if they knew the truth. Just suppose they learned that when praying the Rosary they are actually meditating upon the fifteen central mysteries of Christ's life and applying those mysteries to their own needs. The Blessed Mother has promised that evil will be vanquished and that Her Son will establish peace in the world if enough people pray the Rosary. Terrible, terrible, terrible!

I also want to touch briefly upon two other forms of prayer.

Most people do not recognize these as "prayer." Satan does not want people to understand that both their ordinary labor and sufferings can be offered to God as a form of prayer. Nor does he want them to know that when such an offer is made, especially with charity – out of love for God – the soul receives from Him the remission of sin as well as the grace to persevere in a life of faith and good works. Always discourage people from living in imitation of Jesus. He lived a life of charity, humility, and honest labor.

Yours in darkness,

S corpion

Letter 24

Dear Agent 6,

While Satan has been able to eradicate devotion to the Holy Mother of God in most of the other Christian denominations, supplications for her intercession are still too prevalent in the Catholic community. This is most unfortunate because she does actually have from God the privilege of being a very powerful and effective intercessor. Because God has seen fit to crown her Queen of Heaven and Earth, we demons cringe at the very sight of her. You, too, will learn to keep your distance, and I hope you will not have to learn it the hard way.

Satan strives to destroy the highly privileged practice Catholics have of placing themselves under Mary's mantle of motherly protection and heavenly intercession. One of the ways Catholics exercise this privilege is by wearing the **Scapular**. The Scapular is an extremely powerful weapon against us. Those who wear it with committed attachment to Heaven and with confidence in the promise of eternal life which it carries, profess through it their desire to be united to the Immaculate Heart of Mary. Through the devout wearing of the Scapular a person actually unites his or her heart with that purest of human hearts, the heart of Mary.

Sadly, Agent 6, I must admit to you that when the Scapular and the Rosary come together in a person's life, and especially when they are combined with the practice of **chastity**, Satan's influence becomes so minimal that one might even consider giving up any hope of claiming that soul.

However, the Scapular is only one of the hated **sacramentals** encouraged by the Catholic Church which causes us demons to distance ourselves from those who wear it. There are other painfully effective sacramentals as well. One is **Holy Water**. In the past, Catholic people were quite aware of Holy Water's repulsive nature – that is, its power to dispel a demon's presence. While it is still in common use in churches, fewer and fewer Catholics are keeping it and using it in their homes. Continue to discourage souls from blessing themselves with Holy Water, especially before bed at night and before beginning their day's activities.

Even more repulsive to us is the Crucifix. The Cross is a sacred symbol much hated by Satan, but the Crucifix, because it displays so blatantly the suffering humanity of Christ, is absolutely disdainful to him. Here is what Satan commands us regarding the Crucifix. First, whenever possible discourage the wearing of Crucifixes altogether. However, Satan is realistic enough to realize that if we can't get rid of that sacred symbol entirely, we can at least encourage people to wear only the Cross. The difference between a Crucifix and a Cross is that the Cross is devoid of the Corpus, that is, devoid of the representation of the suffering humanity of Christ.

Second, whether a person wears a Crucifix or a Cross, each is meant to be worn in a manner which places it near to one's heart, but Satan directs us to persuade people to wear these sacramentals in other places on their persons, for example, as one might wear jewelry. You have probably noticed that lately

Satan has been quite successful in promoting the wearing of Crosses, even Crucifixes, as earrings, rings, or merely as ornamental fixtures. It is presently popular to wear large or highly decorative Crosses as a matter of fashion or style. Satan desires this trend to continue for as long as we can possibly keep it going.

The **Miraculous Medal** is another sacramental that places one expressly under Mary's influence and protection. She has promised to obtain through her Son many graces and much help for those who wear it with the proper sentiment. Satan hates the Miraculous Medal, of course, so work hard to discourage your young Catholics from wearing it also.

Before I close, I want to congratulate you on that one case in which you were able to persuade the girl who wanted to imitate her favorite rock star who wears a large Crucifix to remove the Crucifix from her Rosary and wear it on a chain as a fashionable necklace. This caught Satan's attention and it was he who instructed me to compliment you. Had her motivation been to wear the Crucifix as a sign of her Christian **solidarity** and dedication to her Redeemer, you would not have wanted to be so encouraging. However, because her actual motivation was to imitate those who wear the Crucifix in a spirit of mockery, appearing to be what they really are not, you did well to urge her to action.

Yours in darkness,

S corpion

Letter 25

Dear Agent 6,

As I mentioned previously, Satan desires that we discourage the use of all sacramentals, and one of the easiest ways of doing this is to promote the idea that blest sacramentals are neither different nor better than any other symbolic jewelry. Another way to discourage the use of sacramentals is to create the impression that the majority of those who wear or use them are primarily simple-minded and naive.

With the young it is fairly easy to promote the use of alternative symbols, things which appear innocent, but have hidden **occult** influences. Let me show you how even the use of one well-chosen and well-placed symbol can affect an entire generation. A very common and very popular symbol today is the "yin-yang" symbol, a principle from Chinese cosmology. The yin, or feminine passive principle in nature, exhibits darkness, cold, or wetness. The yang, or masculine principle in nature exhibits light, heat, or dryness. Taken together, according to Chinese cosmology, the yin and the yang produce all that comes to be.

Yet, although this popular symbol is rooted in Chinese cosmology, it has an even more hidden occult meaning, one which is explicitly anti-Christian. When this symbol is understood in the way I am about to explain, it is easy to understand why it represents a philosophy highly favored by Satan. The "yin-yang" image was first promoted by Satan through the New Age Movement. Clever as he is, though, he then maneuvered the symbol out of its limited use by New Age advocates and into such popular sports as surfing and the martial arts. Before long, it was not uncommon to see young people of all ages and backgrounds wearing this popular symbol on chains, necklaces, earrings, and T-shirts.

Satan knows that the "yin-yang" symbol secretly promotes the equality of good and evil, good being represented by the white half and evil by the black half. Both of these halves are equal in proportion. Through this imagery, the "yin-yang" symbol supports the highly popular notion that good and evil are a matter of personal perception. In other words, it proposes the misconception that each person decides for himself or herself what is right and what is wrong, what is actually evil and what is actually good. There are no moral absolutes. Good and evil are **relative** to the personal feelings and perceptions of each person, at least this is the false idea which Satan has promoted.

Now, as this popular, but incorrect, notion regarding the relative nature of good and evil has grown, many people have begun to suspect that the passion, death, and resurrection of Jesus Christ – God become man – was an unnecessary action on God's part. Satan has been quite successful in promoting the idea that there was really no necessity for a Redeemer because there was really no evil to overcome in the first place. In other words, evil exists only as people believe it exists and will cease to exist when people cease to believe in its reality. Who needs God? Who needs His grace? A man or a woman can be a good person on his or her own, or at least this is how Satan ultimately seeks to have people believe.

You don't think it is by mere coincidence, do you, that so many young people are attracted to the "all black" clothing look today? It is also not a coincidence that so many are wearing shirts which depict evil themes such as death, skulls, and gore. (Satan has even infiltrated children's games with these evil images.) Neither is it a mere coincidence that young people are being subjected to a media barrage of violence and blatant sexuality. You see, Agent 6, as more and more people accept the proposition that evil is "relative," it becomes easier and easier to deaden their ability to distinguish true goodness from actual evil. Don't you just marvel at the ingenuity of Satan? He is so accomplished at twisting the truth and making wrong appear right that it fills me with exhilaration.

Well, the point I am making with all of this is that Satan wants us to discourage the wearing and use of sacramentals. One of the easiest ways of accomplishing this is to substitute other popular signs, symbols, and designs in their place. Above all, especially work on getting young people to stop wearing their Crucifixes, Scapulars, and Miraculous Medals and to substitute in their place such things as "yin-yang" symbols, peace signs, stars, moons, **ankhs**, skulls, or crystals. Anything is better than those approved, blest sacramentals.

Yours in darkness,

Scorpion

Letter 26

Dear Agent 6,

I am going to reveal to you the remaining deceiver secrets, and these directly involve several of God's commandments. Be clear about what I am going to say next, though, because otherwise all of your work and effort will be rendered fairly ineffective.

A life of committed prayer, especially when it is coupled with daily reflection on the inspired Word of God, evokes God's affection and draws a soul closer and closer to Him, therefore drawing that soul farther and farther away from us. Placing himself or herself under the protection and intercession of Mary and the other saints, as well as the wearing and proper use of blest, approved sacramentals greatly weakens our influence on a soul. Finally, those who participate regularly and devoutly in the Sacraments of Reconciliation and The Eucharist draw to themselves such an abundance of God's merciful graces that Satan is continually aggravated. Unless you disarm souls by effectively discouraging all of these holy practices, the remaining deceiver tactics will be of little use to you.

Now, we'll begin with God's second commandment, "Thou

shalt not take the name of the Lord thy God in vain." It contains within it several avenues by which you can encourage people to offend God.

According to this commandment, God's name must always be pronounced with holy respect and reverence, and it must never be used to express surprise, anger, or impatience, nor to jest, nor is it to be used out of habit. Encourage, therefore, the use of God's name in vain ways, especially the misuse of the name Jesus, God's Son. There was a time when Catholic children were taught to bow their heads when the name Jesus was pronounced. Now many use the name Jesus as a common expression of surprise, disgust, or anger. This is another bad habit we demons encourage!

You may also have noticed, Agent 6, how quickly and easily people of all ages use the expression "I swear to God!" Anyone who swears calls upon God to witness to the truth of what he or she says. Swearing should not be done lightly, but keep your young Catholics thinking that "it's no big deal." Also, by the second commandment people are forbidden to swear falsely, that is, to confirm by oath what they know is not true. Encourage the false idea that it is all right to swear to something one knows is not true as long as one does not get caught. Believe it or not, today it works!

This second commandment also directs people in regard to the taking of vows. A vow is a deliberate promise made to God by which a person binds himself or herself to do something that is especially pleasing to God. Vows must never be made lightly, and they should always be made only after sufficient reflection and with the advice of a prudent **spiritual director**. It doesn't hurt our cause, however, to encourage people, especially young people, to make vows and promises to God one day and to change their minds the next.

Vows also come into play in relationships. If, for example, a person vows to do a good deed or makes a promise to someone, he or she is bound to fulfill that promise. Note, however, that this commandment does not bind evil promises, wicked vows, or baneful oaths, those in which the person swears to do something which is wrong, useless, or contrary to God's laws. Of course, for our purposes, it helps to confuse young people regarding this business of keeping promises, even those involving evil. I once witnessed a case in which a very confused young person vowed to his friends to do an evil deed. Later his conscience assailed him. My agent took quick action and secretly suggested to him that even though his promise was both unreasonable and evil he must not break his vow to his friends because God would be angry with him. Can you believe that this strategy worked?

The point here is that sometimes you may think logically, while these young people are only focusing on their feelings. Play upon their natural tendencies whenever possible.

Yours in darkness,

 corpion

Letter 27

Dear Agent 6,

The third commandment, "Remember thou keep holy the Lord's day," commands the faithful to worship God in a special manner on Sunday, and for Catholics this obligation is fulfilled by assisting at the Holy Sacrifice of the Mass. Satan has been very clever, however, in proposing to Catholic people that they can substitute other forms of worship in place of the Mass. Since I explained to you earlier the reasons for Satan's hatred of the Mass, you can better appreciate the satisfaction he receives when Catholic people leave the Catholic Church altogether or even when they join other Christian denominations. (Fortunately that dreaded reenactment of Calvary – the Holy Sacrifice of the Mass – is omitted in the Protestant churches.)

Another aspect of the third commandment obliges the faithful to refrain from engaging in work or activities that hinder the worship owed to God, the joy proper to the Lord's Day, the performance of the works of mercy, and the appropriate relaxation of mind and body. While certain necessary labor is permitted, the Lord's day is designed to benefit the individual by giving him or her the opportunity to pay more attention to God and to enjoy needed rest and recreation. Lately, however, there has been a growing trend to treat Sunday as any other work day. People are less inclined to pay to God the special attention He has asked for on this day. They are also more inclined to work or participate in affairs of business, commerce, and employment on Sunday, much more than in the past. In some cases work of this nature cannot be helped, but for the most part an increasing number of people are either ignorant of God's commandment, or they think this aspect of His commandment regarding work doesn't matter any more. This is all beneficial to us because the more people are absorbed by the affairs of this world, the less apt they are to set aside time to spend with God through prayer, spiritual reading, or works of charity.

One final point: The Church not only commands the faithful to worship God by assisting at the Holy Sacrifice of the Mass on Sunday or by assisting at a Saturday Vigil Mass, but also on **holy days of obligation**. As you already know, the Holy Sacrifice of the Mass offers an unparalleled opportunity for gaining great spiritual benefits, especially if people participate devoutly. You also know that Satan would, if he could, destroy the Catholic Mass. Even though the Church teaches that Sunday is the day on which the **paschal mystery** is celebrated in light of **apostolic tradition** and is to be observed as the foremost holy day of obligation in the Church throughout the world, Satan has directed us to propose to Catholic people that despite the teaching of the Church, the Mass is an "optional" form of worship. He is not completely satisfied, but he does recognize that some progress has been made. Do the best you can.

Yours in darkness,

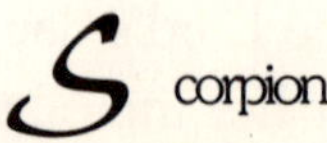

*S*corpion

Letter 28

Dear Agent 6,

Jesus wants His followers to be peacemakers – people of love, kindness, and compassion. Satan wants to turn people into fighters, into vessels of anger, hatred, revenge, drunkenness, and scandal. He has a strong appetite for murder, suicide, euthanasia, and abortion. How do we demons give him what he wants? We encourage people to break God's fifth commandment, "Thou shalt not kill."

The avenues for encouraging people to violate this particular commandment are many. You can, for example, entice your young Catholics into acts of sinful anger. When anger carries with it displeasure great enough to cause a person to desire to punish or hurt the offender, it seriously violates the fifth commandment. You should encourage hatred as well. Hatred is a strong feeling of animosity which combines easily with revenge, the desire to "get even." Revenge stems from anger and evokes the desire for excessive punishment.

Satan also instructs us to encourage both a desire for and a widespread tolerance and acceptance of excessiveness and abuse. Excellent opportunities abound in the areas of excessiveness and abuse – abuse of food, abuse of alcohol, abuse of tobacco, and even the abuse of medicine. He has been particularly interested in having us demons cause many people to incur grave guilt through drunkenness or through a love of speed. Both drunkenness and a love of speed can cause one to put one's own life as well as other people's lives in danger, and exposing oneself or someone else to mortal danger without good reason is a violation of the fifth commandment.

You have probably noticed the appetite people have for drugs of all kinds, an appetite which is overtaking people worldwide. This is one of Satan's greatest success stories, and to make it even better, he has convinced people, especially young people, that it is their own personal right to use illegal, mood-altering substances. He has succeeded in blinding many to the gravely offensive nature of such abuse, so much so that even those who consider themselves "good" can sometimes be persuaded to participate in not only substance abuse, but also in the production of and trafficking in illegal drugs. Satan profoundly appreciates any deceiver who can effectively lead people of any age into the evil practices of using or selling illegal substances. Both are gravely scandalous.

The ability to create scandalous situations which, in turn, bring about scandalous behavior, especially in those who are considered a part of the "flock," is so admired by Satan that it warrants some discussion. Scandal is an attitude, action, or behavior on the part of one person which leads another to sin. If by a certain offensive word or action, or if by the omission of the good a person ought to do, one leads another person into sinful behavior, that person is guilty of scandal. Here is a very workable technique for leading young people into scandal. Encourage them to use the power of negative "peer pressure" in such a way that it leads others to do wrong. Not only can you cause them to be guilty of scandal, but also, they incur responsibility for the evil that they have directly or indirectly encouraged.

Anger, hatred, revenge, substance abuse, excessiveness, and scandalous behavior are pleasing to Satan, but even more pleasing to him are the grave sins of murder, **abortion**, suicide, and euthanasia. These latter are the very kinds of sins Satan lusts after.

Murder is the unjust killing of another human being. Because it is an infringement on the right of God's dominion over human life, murder is a grave sin. The taking of one's life to end his or her suffering, known as euthanasia or "mercy killing," is exactly the kind of sinful behavior Satan advocates because it is gravely contrary to the dignity of the human person and to the respect due to the living God, the Creator.

Also, by God's law, human life must be respected and protected absolutely from the moment of conception. Here is the Church's teaching, and I am quoting from that catechism the Catholic community is so fond of promoting. "Since the first century the Church has affirmed the moral evil of every procured abortion. This teaching has not changed and remains unchangeable. Direct abortion, that is to say, abortion willed either as an end or a means, is gravely contrary to the moral law." Do you know what Satan's attitude is regarding the Church's firm teaching on abortion? Challenge it! Denounce it! Mock it! Deny it! DESTROY IT!

Lastly Agent 6, there is the insidious offense of suicide. We must work very hard to distort the truth that it is God who remains the sovereign Master of life. People are obliged to accept life gratefully and to preserve it for His honor and the salvation of their souls. They are stewards, not owners, of the life God has entrusted to them. Death is not a matter of choice. Each person is responsible to God for his or her life, and God is the sovereign Master of life. Satan wants people to believe that their lives are their concern alone and that they should have the right to live or to die according to their own designs.

What you really want to try to do is to lead a person into a condition of hopelessness which appears to have no solution. I will provide you with a typical pattern to follow. It is a pattern that has proven successful in the past, especially in the recent past. First, manipulate the person to get into situations which entice him or her into gravely serious sins. Sexual relationships before marriage, abortion, and drug abuse have shown the greatest potential for inducing states of serious depression and hopelessness, so stick with these whenever possible. Once a person has fallen into any of these grace-destroying behaviors and with your aid begins to slip into depression, do whatever you can to enhance the guilt mechanism. Usually it is better to repress guilt after sin so the person is not moved to repentance, but in potential suicide cases you want to maliciously twist the role of guilt and use it to your best advantage. While magnifying the feelings of guilt, the next thing you'll want to do is to trick the person into thinking that he or she cannot possibly confess certain sins.

Next, further intensify the person's feelings of hopelessness and despair, and especially do what you can to convince the young person that there is no one who cares or understands what he or she is going through. Discourage any real communication of the seriousness of the problem to his or her parents, teachers, clergy, or counselors. After that – promote thoughts of suicide, constant thoughts of suicide.

I'm sure you recognize that a person who can be brought to the point of such despair as to commit suicide will have denied God the opportunity He desires to forgive the soul and lavish on it His mercy and assistance. Remember, however, that grave psychological disturbances, anguish, or grave fear of hardship, suffering, or torture can diminish the responsibility of the one commiting suicide. By ways known to Him alone, God <u>can</u> provide the opportunity for salutary repentance. While Satan's never ending lust for destroying human life is difficult to satisfy, this kind of treachery against human souls comes very close to giving him what he wants. You will do well to heed my advice in this matter.

Yours in darkness,

S corpion

Letter 29

Dear Agent 6,

The whole prospect of drug abuse has proven to be such a powerful and effective tool for destroying human lives and human souls that it deserves its own commentary.

First of all, let's not forget that in the majority of cases the decision to use illegal substances (The use of alcohol by minors is included here.) is a conscious choice which violates both the fourth and fifth commandments. Occasionally young people can be innocently initiated into substance abuse by ill-intentioned adults, even one's own parents, but with the educational and informational resources available today, it is unlikely that any school-aged child or teenager does not know that taking illegal drugs is both disobedient and harmful.

Master deceiver that he is, however, Satan has been able to neutralize the efforts of health educators and concerned parents chiefly by the very nature of the drugs themselves. You must understand, Agent 6, that precisely because of the way drugs work, because at first they can seem to be very helpful, very effective, and very pleasurable, they often become a friend to the young person, rather than the deadly enemy that they truly are. This is the "trick" of drugs, that they usually string a person along allowing him or her to feel "in charge" just long enough for addiction to set in. By the time his or her mind, body, soul, school work, relationships, friendships, and family life begin to collapse, he or she is "hooked." Of course in the case of certain drugs, such as "crack" cocaine, addiction can occur even after the first or second use. Needless to say, Satan loves "crack."

We've got young people right where Satan wants them when they are dependent and desperate, feeling like there is nowhere to turn except to begin looking for more potent, and therefore, more addictive substances to ease their pain. Satan has used the scientific knowledge and expertise of people whom he has corrupted to provide a wide variety of methods for producing and using illegal substances, as well as to concoct a whole string of very strong, very powerful, highly addictive synthetic drugs known as "designer" drugs.

Here is a deceiver secret that all demons must know but that people must never understand. Mood-altering, mind-altering drugs mimic within the human heart and soul the very relationship of love that God Himself wishes to have with each of His children. Intimacy with God, wherein a person shares in God's very life and in which God abides sensibly in the heart and soul of that person by the presence of His own Spirit, is absolutely the most fulfilling experience that a human creature can have in this world. But such a life is found only after a surrender of oneself to God is made without reservation, and this is usually accomplished only after sincere repentance leads one to a life of intimate, dedicated, committed prayer and works of charity. God is true to His promises. To those who live their lives for Him, He has promised a peace which the world cannot give. Believe me, Agent 6, He delivers!

Drugs, on the other hand, offer the human heart and soul

an experience similar in some respects to the relationship one wishes to have with God. However, these experiences are counterfeit and achieved without the effort it takes to be the recipient of God's real gifts of love and peace. Drugs can only offer the experiences of counterfeit love, counterfeit peace, and counterfeit fulfillment. At first, drug-induced experiences can have all the appearances of what the human heart and soul craves, but these experiences have none of the actual substance to deliver the life the individual is really seeking. Drug abuse offers only a life of empty, unfulfilled, life-destroying promises.

There is another reason why Satan desires us to encourage drug abuse. Drugs undermine the ability of one's conscience to guide decisions and behavior choices. Under the influence of mind-altering substances, alcohol included, the conscience becomes very dull, knocking out both the consideration of future consequences as well as the fear of offending Almighty God. Once drug addiction sets in, the above considerations are barely even perceptible factors in a person's decision-making process.

Satan also wants us to do whatever we can to render ineffective the substance abuse prevention information which is offered to young people. Remember, Satan does not want young people to understand the "trick" of drugs, the fact that at first drugs can seem to have a good effect. Nor does he want them to understand that uncomfortable feelings are experienced by everybody and are a natural part of life. He also does not want young people to develop the skills they need to cope with the emotional difficulties all people are apt to face at one time or another in their lives.

You see, Agent 6, we do not want young people prepared to deal with the reality of uncomfortable feelings. We do not want them to possess the character and fortitude to see difficulties and frustrations through without the aid of chemicals. We want them to believe that life is supposed to be all fun as opposed to a blend of enjoyment with work, self-discipline, and consistent application of effort to achieve goals. Satan wants tension-relieving, enjoyment-producing, mood-altering, life-destroying substances to play a major role in people's lives. Do whatever you must, therefore, to give him what he wants!

Yours in darkness,

S corpion

Letter 30

Dear Agent 6,

There are two commandments against which Satan has waged an all-out affront: The sixth commandment, "Thou shalt not commit **adultery**," and the ninth commandment, "Thou shalt not **covet** thy neighbor's wife." You must excel in the great art of "sexual deception" if you desire Satan's true regard.

In essence, Agent 6, the human body is God's masterpiece, the work of His hands, designed as the dwelling place of His presence and His grace. God has a jealous regard for His masterpiece. He does not want to see it soiled and degraded, reduced to an instrument of indecent pleasures. So, what is our most expedient course of action? Encourage all kinds of immoral activity, such as impure and unchaste speech, and especially encourage people to look at things, persons, or pictures (still or animated) which can arouse the sexual appetite and produce lustful desires.

There is a wide variety of avenues by which people can be enticed into immoral thoughts, words, and deeds. Indecent books, romantic novels, tantalizing television programs, and scandalous movies depicting sinful sexual love and sinful sexual relationships have become a huge money-making industry, an industry which attracts people of all ages. News tabloids, magazines, and pornographic materials with lewd pictures and sensational sexual liaisons are accessible even to the young. Obscene television programs, video cassettes, movies, and music videos abound. At the same time, fewer and fewer people see the extremely offensive nature of these things.

The infiltration of Satan's philosophy of lust into the music industry has created for us a virtual feast of moral corruption upon which to feed. Additionally, Satan has created within countless numbers of people a sinful curiosity which desires to know everything, see everything, experience everything, and try everything.

Satan expressly desires his agents to promote immodesty and indecency in all levels of society. One way of doing this is through clothing. To wear clothing that is sexually alluring, sexually revealing, tight to the body, or scant in its covering constitutes transgressions against the level of modesty God commands of His people. However, while it is useful to encourage your young people to reveal their bodies through immodest dress and behavior, you also want to carefully conceal from them the fact that to be a source of temptation through immodest or indecent exposure of one's body is also to become guilty of the sin of impurity. There appears to be a growing lack of awareness that what one wears, how one looks, even the way in which one sits can become an occasion of sin for oneself or another person. Satan wants us to reinforce this trend because immodesty leads to offenses against the ninth commandment which calls for **purity** of thought and desire.

Because Satan hates purity, he demands that his demons contrive in all ways possible to destroy the virtue of purity. Satan's hatred of purity is understandable in light of the fact that it is the pure in heart, those who attune their intellects and their wills to the demands of God's holiness, that have been given the promise of seeing God face to face. In other words, purity of heart is a precondition for the vision of God. Purity of heart enables one to see the human body (one's own as well as one's neighbor's) as God sees it – as a temple of the Holy Spirit, a manifestation of divine beauty, and a creation of His hand which demands great respect. Is it any wonder why Satan goes to extreme lengths to destroy the virtue of purity and to place it in a position of great disfavor?

Another strategy Satan instructs us to use is the promotion of moral permissiveness. Through moral permissiveness, a lack of discipline over one's desires, feelings, and imagination can be created. A lack of discipline then leads to a condition of unrestrained sexuality, a condition which degrades the moral and spiritual dignity of the human person.

Chief among the offenses against the modesty, chastity, and purity called for by God's sixth and ninth commandments are lust, **masturbation**, **fornication**, **pornography**, prostitution, homosexuality, and adultery. These are deeply serious offenses.

Incidentally, I was impressed with your manipulation of that young girl at the party. What she would never have done sober was almost too easy after a few hours of drinking. Her guilt may cause her to want to go to confession. Discourage that idea! Get her together with her new "love" as soon as possible. We don't want those two cooling off.

Remember this: The younger people are when they become entrapped by sins which violate purity, modesty, and chastity, the easier it is to keep them in bondage throughout the entire course of their lives.

Yours in darkness,

Scorpion

Letter 31

Dear Agent 6,

Satan has brilliantly concocted a belief within society regarding certain "rights" that individuals have. One of the principal bogus rights he has advanced is the "right to sin," and to do so without consequence. He has fabricated the incredibly unfounded belief that if one determines for oneself, according to one's circumstances, present needs, or particular feelings, that sinful behavior is the most practical or most expedient course of action, then the sinful behavior is somehow "magically" erased and will not count against the person.

The young people with whom you are working have been what I might call "nourished" on just this kind of propaganda. Thanks to this treacherous distortion of truth by our most admired "father of lies," Satan, you will now find many of the younger generation who, in one way or another, demand the right to sin if it gets them what they want or where they want to go. (Where they usually want to go is to the "top," but the so-called "top" is just an illusion introduced by Satan ages ago.)

Where am I heading with all of this? There is a particular "right" that Satan has advanced. Huge numbers of people have been trapped by his web of trickery. It is the claim that people have the "right to a trial marriage." This idea of a right to live together before marriage is such a clever masquerade of supposed common sense and practicality, that it is impossible to imagine what better decoy Satan could have set out to allure the unsuspecting millions for whom this particular trap was meant.

Be clear on God's moral law, Agent 6. Sexual intimacy must take place exclusively within marriage. Sexual union outside of marriage constitutes a grave sin against the sixth commandment. It is a sin so grave it excludes one from sacramental communion, but encourage people to ignore this fact.

Even where there is an intention of getting married later, living together and having sexual relations before marriage are both prohibited. You will recall that God really does love His people, and because He loves them, He desires what is in their best interest. The fact is that "trial marriages" are not in the best interest of those involved because such relationships cannot receive from God the sacramental blessings and graces necessary for faithfulness. God knows this, of course, but so does Satan. While God desires what is best for His people, Satan desires what can ultimately destroy them.

Not only are such trial unions devoid of God's approval and grace, living together before marriage, even with the intention of marrying in the future, is a form of "tempting God." It is like saying to God, "I demand the rights, privileges, and advantages of the married state (Some even expect His blessing!), but I refuse to submit to the standards You have established for a man and a woman to be legitimately united in Your sight.

One of our slyest deceptions has been to conceal the truth that the family is the original cell of social life. It is the natural society in which husband and wife are called to give themselves in love and in the gift of life. The family is the community in which, from childhood, one can learn moral values, begin to honor God, and make good use of freedom. Since human love demands a total and definitive gift of persons to one another, it cannot tolerate "trial marriages." Nor do such arrangements bring forth the true good of the persons involved or of the children that may issue from such relationships. People believe that they can, in a certain sense, cheat God. He has ordained the act of sexual union to achieve certain good things, but those good things can only be brought to their fullness when they are enacted within the conditions He requires.

One of the *goods* God has placed within the sexual union is the bonding it causes when the two persons become one flesh. This physical bond is designed to help strengthen the mental, emotional, and spiritual bonds of the relationship. A second *good* which God has placed within sexual union is the ability of the man and the woman to actively cooperate with God in bringing forth a new human being. When, through sexual union, a new human being is created, God creates a new living soul.

It should be noted, however, that the *goods* which God has purposely attached to the act of sexual union (bonding and babies) can only be experienced in the fulfilling and wonderful way God intended for them to be experienced when they are attained through a loving marital commitment of husband and wife.

It amazes me that young people are surprised when, having taken part in what is the most intimate form of physical union God has given to them, they often cannot just walk away as if it was "no big deal." Of course it's a big deal! But then, this is part of the lie about sex that Satan commands us to encourage. He wants people of all ages to believe that having sex outside of covenanted marriage is "no big deal." By the way, a very high percentage of the young people who have committed suicide once believed that lie.

Yours in darkness,

S corpion

Letter 32

Dear Agent 6,

We will now examine the intentions and desires of the heart which God's tenth commandment, "Thou shalt not covet thy neighbor's goods," enjoins upon the faithful. In doing so, you will discover what I call the "short road to a barren spirit." You will also see that it is through the corrupt desires of the heart that a person can be more quickly misdirected in ways which violate God's seventh commandment, "Thou shalt not steal."

First, since the tenth commandment forbids greed and the desire to amass earthly goods without limit, you will want to begin at a very early age to inspire in the hearts of the young a hunger and thirst for the possession of "things," especially what they consider the "right" things. In the earliest years, you can begin to develop this hunger and nourish this thirst by encouraging the constant flow of newer and better toys and playthings along with greater and more exciting amusements into the lives of young people. Given the mass media advertising campaigns and the consistency by which young people are stimulated to believe that having the "right things" produces happiness, the stage is then set for a widespread condition of one of Satan's favorite sins, envy. Envy, Agent 6, is one of the **capital sins**, and it is worth whatever effort it may take to encourage it.

Envy refers to the sadness one feels at the sight of what another owns or possesses. Envy moves the heart to desire to acquire the goods of another, even if doing so calls for dishonest or unjust behavior. Envy is often at the root of the very offenses prohibited by the seventh commandment. Satan desires people to harbor envious feelings because through this capital sin they can be enticed to steal, to cheat, to unfairly keep for oneself what rightly belongs to others, to damage another's property, to fail to pay one's debts, or to participate in bribery. Through envy, as well as through greed, employers can be encouraged to deny laborers a just wage, and employees can be encouraged to waste time on the job, work carelessly, neglect to take reasonable care of their employer's property, or to use the employer's property or resources for their own personal needs.

The best approach is to start small because small acts of dishonesty eventually turn into bigger ones. Encourage the following ideas. Start with this one: *A little cheating is all right. It's only the big cheating that's wrong.* Also push this idea: *Since so many people cheat today it's really not considered as serious a sin as it used to be.* Another falsehood to use is: *Stealing or cheating, especially in small ways, only counts against the person if he or she gets caught.*

Beating the system in clever ways must be made to appear to young people as a virtue rather than a major defect in one's character. Whatever it takes to get ahead, or as I mentioned previously, to get to the "top," must be represented to young people as a justifiable reason to cheat, steal, or behave in dishonest ways.

There is a certain disposition of the heart, however, that God especially appreciates, and it is just this type of disposition we must work against. Because an unselfish, charitable, generous disposition of heart was so highly praised by Jesus, Satan despises this attitude and has a very deep disdain for charitable people. The oppressed and the poor of the world elicit Jesus's compassion because He willingly took poverty upon Himself and identified Himself with the least of His brethren. God's seventh commandment calls the faithful to imitate Jesus's love and compassion for the less fortunate members of society, but Satan's policy is to encourage immoderate attachment to riches combined with selfishness so that people become unwilling to share their resources. He also wants us to encourage self-centeredness, thus reducing any sense of personal responsibility toward the poor.

Remember, Agent 6, it is basically by envy that Satan and those of us who are aligned with him are motivated to seek the destruction of human souls. They are the ones destined to take the places in Heaven which we should have had. You have probably noticed certain tendencies in yourself. Do you have, for example, a tendency to feel strongly satisfied at the sight of a soul's misfortune or to feel uncontrollable resentment at the sight of a soul's prosperity, especially good fortune in spiritual matters? This is exactly the attitude you must perpetuate in those to whom you have been assigned. It is the model of Satan, after all, and what better model does a demon have?

Yours in darkness,

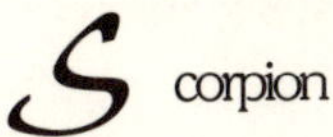 corpion

Letter 33

Dear Agent 6,

As I near the completion of my instructions, I must warn you again about Mary, Christ's mother, and the role that she plays as **advocate** and protectress of souls. She is truly a creature formed and molded by the hand of God Himself, and her formation was in the manner befitting one who was to be His mother. She was formed in a most pure way, and in her formation she was endowed with all of the virtues and perfections which the **Triune God** personally infused into her soul. Besides being enriched with all of these virtues, she was also afforded the privilege of communicating, in accordance with the Divine Will of God, the graces and favors necessary for human souls, especially for those who invoke her as her children. The Triune God gave and conferred upon her the right of distributing the treasures of Divine Mercy. She has from God the privilege of enriching the needy, of obtaining the graces necessary to free sinners, and of acting as a universal refuge for all men, women, and children. In addition, God desires that people recognize her as their Heavenly Mother and as the Mediatrix (distributor) of the infinite bounties of God. Above all, she was given dominion and power over Satan and over all his allied demons. It is for this reason, Agent 6, that we fear her presence and her name. Because of her, our deceits are exposed, and our projects are crushed and annihilated. She is a refuge in which the faithful can find protection from the dread of the demons and their snares.

She prays with great love for souls and intercedes for them before the Throne of God, soliciting and procuring for them eternal life, especially for those, who in the course of their lives, commend themselves to her care. When she intercedes for souls before God, nothing is denied to her. She has the power to command Satan and to keep him away from souls, and she has at her disposal the arm of the Almighty.

Because this beloved woman defends those souls who devoutly call on her for help and who distinguish themselves in their devotion, **veneration**, and love for her, Satan commands us to do all in our power to destroy the truth about the role God has entrusted to her. The fewer the Christians who place themselves under her protection, the better it is for us, for after God, the Blessed Virgin Mary is Satan's chief adversary.

Yours in darkness,

S corpion

Letter 34

Dear Agent 6,

I would like to be ending these letters on a note of triumph, but unfortunately I must end them on a note of caution. We have another formidable foe among the Heavenly Court, and I feel obligated to warn you of the opposition presented by this one whose position carries great power against us.

St. Michael, the great Archangel, is represented by the Church as holding the highest place among the angels. The Church refers to him as "Prince of Heavenly Hosts." The Church tells of the glories of this great Archangel in several portions of Her **Liturgy** and presents him chiefly as the Head of God's armies, champion of the people of God in the Old Testament, and the powerful guardian of God's chosen flock under the New Covenant. His name, "Michael," means "Who is like God." Whenever some act of wondrous power must be performed, Michael is usually sent to make it clear that no one can do what God does.

It is not by coincidence that St. Michael is represented in art as the angel warrior, the conqueror of Lucifer, the one who sets his heel upon Satan's head and threatens him with his sword, the one who pierces Satan with his lance and is prepared to chain him down in the great abyss, in the hellish regions from where he will not issue after the last day.

Glowing zeal for the honor of God is St. Michael's distinctive trait and virtue. He has proven himself a valiant warrior for the honor of God, both in Heaven and on earth. St. Michael will not fail to come to the aid of the Catholic Church in these modern days just as he did not fail to do so in the days of old. If the faithful fervently and confidently implore him to do so, he will defend them. This is why we must defeat this enemy of ours by creating a condition of ignorance and indifference regarding this great and powerful ally of the Church. It is he who waged the first battle against Lucifer and vanquished him. It is he who, when the end of the world draws near, will wage a final battle against the **Antichrist** and protect those who are earnest seekers of the truth from Satan's fiercest and most powerful forces of seduction.

Although many of the faithful recognize that in these, their own times, the condition of the world is critical, we do not want them to recognize the great potential for help and assistance that can be gained through the intercession of St. Michael and the faithful angels. If people come to the full realization that God has appointed St. Michael as the special defender and advocate of Christians against Satanic powers, they will readily place themselves under his protection and begin invoking his assistance for the Church and for individual souls.

I dare not even contemplate the effect that the intercession of this powerful champion for the honor of God, who is also the defender of the Catholic Faith, could have on our ability to corrupt and destroy human souls. If we lose our influence over great numbers of souls, our own battle could be irreversibly lost!

I will be monitoring the progress you are making with your young Catholics. Be assured that you will hear from me again.

Yours in darkness,

S corpion

Glossary of Terms

ABORTION – Induced termination of a pregnancy.

ABSOLUTION – The freeing of a person from his or her sins by Jesus through the priest who hears confession.

ADULTERY – Voluntary sexual intercourse between a married person and a partner other than the lawful spouse.

ADVOCATE – One who intercedes (speaks in favor of) on another's behalf.

ANKH – An ancient symbol for fertility and reincarnation.

ANTICHRIST – The English term from the Greek *antichristos* meaning "against Christ" or "adversary of Christ."

APOSTLES – The twelve men chosen by Jesus who taught and presided over the early Church and spoke in Jesus's Name.

APOSTOLIC TRADITION – The teachings of Jesus witnessed

by the Apostles and passed on to their successors, who were guided by the Holy Spirit.

BENEDICTION – The ceremony of solemn adoration of Jesus in the Eucharist in which the priest blesses the people with the Consecrated Host enclosed in a sacred vessel called a Monstrance, which is visible to the worshiping community.

BESTOW – To present as a gift in recognition of an honor conferred.

BISHOP – From the Greek *episkopos* (overseer), the bishop is a successor of the Apostles. Upon a bishop is conferred the highest degree of holy orders. He has full jurisdiction over his diocese and is directly responsible to the Pope.

CAPITAL SINS – Seven inclinations or tendencies toward sin. (See Appendix.)

CALUMNIATING – Causing harm to another's good name through lies.

CATHOLIC CHURCH – The community called into being by Jesus Himself. The Catholic Church has been understood in every period of her history as a living community, many members united by one Faith, professing one doctrine, sharing the same seven sacraments, and governed by the Vicar of Christ on earth (the Pope) and the successors to the Apostles.

CHANNELING OF SPIRIT GUIDES – A dangerous New Age practice in which it is believed a human being becomes the spokesperson for a "spirit guide."

CHANNELS – (in the New Age Movement) Hypersensitive humans through which spirit guides are believed to speak. Such individuals are more than likely being duped by Satan's demons.

CHARACTER – (in Catholicism) A lasting spiritual seal or mark that expresses consecration.

CHASTITY – The virtue of those who keep the sixth and ninth commandments. Also, the name of one of the vows made by those in religious life which involves giving up marriage and family life.

CHOIRS – On the basis of references to them in the Bible, angels are traditionally ranked in a celestial hierarchy of nine orders – Seraphim, Cherubim, Thrones, Dominions, Powers, Virtues, Principalities, Archangels, and Angels.

CHURCH'S LAWS (PRECEPTS OF THE CHURCH) – Special duties which we, as Catholics, are expected to obey and fulfill. (See Appendix.)

CLERGY – Men who are ordained ministers of the Church (Deacons, Priests, Bishops.)

COMMANDMENTS – The Ten Commandments communicated to Moses by God on Mt. Sinai. These laws were given to us by God to help us live in a way worthy of our dignity as human beings and as His children.

CONFER – To bestow.

CONSCIENCE – The function of the human intellect when it

makes moral judgments.

CONSECRATION – The most important moment of the Mass, in which Jesus, acting through the ordained priest, changes bread and wine into His Body and Blood.

COVENANT – An agreement and a commitment made between God and His people to fulfill the mandates of the pact contracted, for example, in the Ten Commandments. Covenants can also be ties made between persons, for example, in marriage.

COVET – To feel envious desire for that which is another's. To wish for excessively and longingly.

CRYSTALS – Transparent, colorless, or color-tinted glass segments of superior quality, falsely believed by certain people to be endowed with powerful attributes or characteristics that can help one "tune in" to the universal life force.

DEMONS – Evil spirits. In Christianity, the angels who followed Lucifer's act of prideful disobedience toward God and were removed from their exalted position and cast into Hell. God, however, permits them to tempt human beings in a limited way in order to test our loyalty and fidelity to Him.

DEVOUT – Deeply religious.

DISSENSION – A difference of opinion, especially one that leads to argument or strife.

DOCTRINE [OF THE CATHOLIC CHURCH] – The Doctrine

of the Catholic Church comprises all those teachings in faith and morals entrusted to the Church by Christ through the Apostles and given for the sake of our salvation.

EUCHARIST – The sacrament of Jesus's complete presence, body, blood, soul, and divinity, in which, under the appearances of bread and wine, He offers His sacrifice again, comes to His people as our spiritual food, and remains in our midst to be close to us and help us.

EXAMINATION OF CONSCIENCE – Reflection for the purpose of discovering or recalling sins committed.

FORNICATION – Sexual intercourse between unmarried people. A sin against the sixth and ninth commandments.

GIFTS OF THE HOLY SPIRIT – Seven special helps from the Holy Spirit that keep us ready to recognize and use His actual graces. The gifts are – Wisdom, Understanding, Right Judgment, Courage/Fortitude, Knowledge, Piety/Reverence, and Holy Fear of the Lord. (See Appendix.)

GRACE – Unmerited divine assistance given to people for their regeneration or sanctification. A state of sanctification enjoyed through divine grace. A virtue coming from God.

GUARDIAN ANGEL – A heavenly spirit assigned by God to watch over each individual during life. The role of the Guardian Angel is both to guide the person to good thoughts, works, and words, and to preserve him or her from evil.

HELL – The place, state, or condition prepared for Satan, his subjects, and the unrepentant for all eternity.

HOLY DAYS OF OBLIGATION – Certain days besides Sundays on which Catholics are expected to take part in the Mass. These days are – Christmas (Dec. 25), Solemnity of the Mother of God (Jan. 1), Ascension Thursday, the Assumption (Aug. 15), All Saints Day (Nov 1) and the Immaculate Conception (Dec. 8).

HOLY ORDERS – The sacrament through which Jesus gives His Spirit to men to make them Deacons, Priests, and Bishops and gives them powers that belong to each office.

HOLY WATER – Water blessed by a priest in order to give God's blessing to those who use it.

HUMILITY – A supernatural virtue that forms the basis of all good actions because it acknowledges our total dependence on God and our obligation to serve and be lovingly obedient to Him. Humility opens us to the grace of God because a humble person gives God the credit for the good that he or she does. Thus a humble person can better resist temptations than one who does not possess this virtue.

IMMORAL – Contrary to Christian principles.

IMPULSIVENESS – The inclination to respond or act suddenly.

INCARNATION – The central mystery of Christianity is the doctrine that in union with His divine nature, the Second Person of the Holy Trinity, the Son of God, assumed our human nature body and soul, and he was born of the Virgin Mary to live among us in order to accomplish the work of our redemption.

LAWFUL SUPERIORS – Those whom God has willed, after Him, that we should honor, such as our parents, teachers, and all those invested with authority for our good.

LITURGY – The Church's public worship. It includes all the rites and ceremonies by which the Church expresses her worship of God.

LUST – An intense desire or longing.

MAGISTERIUM – Th e teaching office of the Church. To safeguard the real substance of faith in Jesus Christ and to prevent the individual from being left on his or her own, the Magisterium of the Church was established by Christ. The Church takes the teachings of Christ and the doctrines taught by the Apostles, hands them down faithfully with the assistance of the Holy Spirit, and calls upon all to place their faith in these teachings.

MASS – The sacrifice of the Cross taking place today on our altars. A memorial of Jesus's death, resurrection, and ascension. A holy covenant meal in which we receive Jesus Himself.

MASTURBATION – The erotic stimulation of the genital organs by manual or other bodily contact exclusive of sexual intercourse. A sin against God's sixth commandment.

MIRACULOUS MEDAL – On November 27, 1830 the Blessed Virgin Mary appeared to St. Catherine Laboure of the Daughters of Charity in Paris, France. The Blessed Mother asked that a medal be made in honor of her Immaculate Conception saying, "Have the medal struck after this model. (St. Catherine saw an image of what the medal should look like.) All who wear it will receive great graces. They should wear it around the neck."

MORTAL SIN – A serious offense against God which drives sanctifying grace out of the soul.

NEW AGE MOVEMENT – A movement designed to remove God as transcendent, supreme Creator and replace Him with a god of pantheistic nature. A movement which believes and teaches that all men and women are potential "gods."

NEW COVENANT – The New Testament Covenant is a new pledge in Christ's blood. Our relationship with God as Father is sealed through Jesus's death and resurrection and His gift of the Holy Spirit Who is given to us in Baptism.

OBSCENE – Offensive to acceptable standards of decency. Inciting lustful feelings; lewd. Offensive or repulsive to Christian morality; loathsome.

OCCULT – Matters regarded as involving the action or influences of supernatural agencies or some secret knowledge of them. Christians are warned to shun the occult.

ORIGINAL SIN – The lack of sanctifying grace with which each of us comes into the world because our first parents, Adam and Eve, lost grace both for themselves and for us.

OSTENSORIUM – The sacred vessel used for exposition and adoration of the Blessed Sacrament, otherwise known as a Monstrance.

OUIJA BOARDS – Boards with the alphabet and other signs on them that are used to seek spiritualistic or telepathic messages. In Christianity, these boards are considered a dangerous practice by which contact with demons is often mistakenly believed to be in contact with deceased members of the human family.

PASCHAL MYSTERY – God's love and salvation revealed to us through the life, passion, death, resurrection, and glorification of His Son, Jesus Christ.

PENANCE – Prayers or good works to make up for sin.

PENITENT – A person receiving the Sacrament of Reconciliation.

POPE – A term referring exclusively to the Roman Pontiff, called His Holiness the Pope, who governs the Universal Church as the successor of St. Peter.

PORNOGRAPHY – The depiction of erotic behavior in pictures, film, or writing intended to cause sexual excitement. Pornography constitutes a grave sin against God's sixth and ninth commandments.

PRAYER – Speaking to God with mind and heart, and often, with voice as well.

PRIEST – A man who has received the Sacrament of Holy Orders which imprints on his soul a "character," lasting forever, signifying a special sharing in the priesthood of Christ and which gives him the power and grace to perform the sacred duties required of a priest.

PRINCIPAL EFFECTS OF ORIGINAL SIN – People find it harder to do good and to live in harmony with God's laws. There is an inclination to evil which must be resisted, and this weakness or tendency to sin, is a result of the "original sin" of our first parents, Adam and Eve.

PURGATORY – A condition of suffering (cleansing) after death in which souls make up for their sins before entering Heaven.

PURITY – The virtue by which we avoid immoral thoughts, words, and actions and cultivate the virtue of chastity.

RECOLLECTION – A person who practices recollection turns his or her attention inward, ignoring distractions and activities that can turn his or her attention away from God.

REINCARNATION – An erroneous theory of rebirth in new bodies or forms of life. In the New Age Movement, it refers to the rebirth of souls into new human bodies.

RELATIVE – Not absolute; independent.

RELIGIOUS LIFE – A life in which Christian men or women consecrate themselves to God and to the work of His Kingdom by taking vows of poverty, chastity, and obedience. Ordinarily, those serving God in religious life live together in a religious community and are dedicated to some specific ministry like social work, care of the sick, religious education, teaching, preaching, or missionary work.

REPARATION – Making up for one's own sins or those of others.

REPENTANT – The state of being sorry for sins and having the intention not to sin again.

ROSARY – A "Gospel Prayer" made up of Our Fathers, Hail Marys, and Glorias in which we think about important events in the lives of Jesus and Mary. It is composed of 15 decades which are divided into the joyful, sorrowful, and glorious mysteries.

SACRAMENT – An effective sign of grace, instituted by Christ and entrusted to the Church, by which divine life is dispensed to us.

SACRAMENTALS – Those objects, actions, prayers and the like which help us become aware of Christ's presence in our lives. Sacramentals prepare us for the all-important signs of Christ's grace, the sacraments.

SACRILEGE – Violent, contemptuous, or disrespectful treatment of persons or objects dedicated to the service of God. Also, receiving sacraments unworthily and in a state of mortal sin.

SANCTIFYING GRACE – The grace (gift of God) that enables us to share in the nature and life of God and makes us holy. It is distinguished from actual grace which is a temporary help from God that is given to us at the moment of temptation.

SATAN – The name attributed to Lucifer, the fallen angel, who because of sinful pride and disobedience was cast from his exalted position into Hell.

SCAPULAR – Two small pieces of cloth, fastened by strings and worn around the neck in front and in back as a sacramental (the most common one being in honor of Mary as Our Lady Of Mount Carmel.)

SELF-INDULGENCE – Excessive gratification of one's desires.

SOLIDARITY – Unity (as of a group or class) that produces or is based upon community of interests, objectives, and standards.

SPIRITUAL COMMUNION – The belief in the real presence of Jesus in the Eucharist and the desire to receive Him supernaturally when one cannot receive the Sacred Host.

SPIRITUAL DIRECTOR – A person who is skilled in Spiritual Theology and assists a person to discover God's Will in his or her life and helps that person to follow it along the road to Christian perfection.

SPONSOR – A caring role model for how a Christian lives. Sponsors at Baptism have the responsibility of watching over the religious education of the child baptized. Sponsors at Confirmation are to see that the confirmed person acts as a true witness to Christ and faithfully fulfills the obligations connected with this sacrament.

STATE OF GRACE – A soul in the state of possessing sanctifying grace.

STEREOTYPE – An oversimplified opinion that is thought to be typical of any person, group, event, or issue.

SUPERNATURAL – Above and beyond what is natural. Having to do with God's grace.

TAROT CARDS – A deck of 22 pictorial playing cards used for fortune-telling. A dangerous occult practice.

TRIUNE GOD – Refers to the Christian belief that God is one infinite divine nature in which three persons, Father, Son, and Holy Spirit, totally possess the one nature.

UFOs – Unidentified Flying Objects. In the New Age Movement, manifestations wrongly believed to be spaceships of various sizes and shapes in which it is believed that extraterrestrials sometimes visit earth.

VENERATION – Devotion to and invocation of the saints.

VENIAL SIN – Personal sin which weakens but does not kill our relationship with God.

VIRTUES – Habits which incline us to do good. (See Appendix.)

WORTHY COMMUNION – Reception of the Eucharist in a state free from mortal sin, with a right intention, and in obedience to the Church's laws on the fast before receiving Communion.

Appendix

THE SIGN OF THE CROSS

In the name of the Father,
and of the Son, and of the
Holy Spirit. Amen.

THE OUR FATHER

Our Father,
Who art in heaven,
hallowed be Thy Name.
Thy Kingdom come,
Thy Will be done on earth
as it is in heaven.
Give us this day
our daily bread,
and forgive us our trespasses,
as we forgive those
who trespass against us.
And lead us not into temptation,
but deliver us from evil.
Amen.

THE HAIL MARY

Hail Mary, full of Grace,
The Lord is with Thee.
Blessed are thou among women,
and blessed is the fruit
of thy womb, Jesus.
Holy Mary, Mother of God,
pray for us sinners,
now and at the our of our death.
Amen.

GLORY BE

Glory be to the Father, and to the Son,
and to the Holy Spirit.
As it was in the beginning,
is now, and ever shall be,
world without end.
Amen.

APOSTLE'S CREED

I believe in God, the Father Almighty,
Creator of heaven and earth;
and in Jesus Christ, His only Son, Our Lord;
Who was conceived by the Holy Spirit,
born of the Virgin Mary,
suffered under Pontius Pilate,
was crucified, died and was buried.
He descended into hell; the third day
He arose again from the dead;
He ascended into heaven,
sits at the right hand of God
the Father Almighty;
from thence He shall come to judge
the living and the dead.
I believe in the Holy Spirit,
The Holy Catholic Church,
the communion of saints,
the forgiveness of sins,
the resurrection of the body,
and life everlasting.
Amen.

PRAYER TO OUR GUARDIAN ANGEL

Angel of God, my guardian dear,
to whom God's love commits me here;
Ever this day be at my side
to light and guard, to rule and guide.
Amen.

THE MEMORARE

Remember, O most gracious Virgin Mary,
that never was it known that anyone
who fled to thy protection,
implored thy help, or sought thy intercession
was left unaided.
Inspired with this confidence,
I fly unto thee, O Virgin of virgins, my Mother.
To thee I come; before thee I stand, sinful and sorrowful.
O Mother of the Word Incarnate,
despise not my petitions, but in thy mercy
hear and answer them. Amen.

HAIL, HOLY QUEEN

Hail, Holy Queen, Mother of Mercy,
our life, our sweetness and our hope.
To thee do we cry, poor banished children of Eve;
to thee do we send up our sighs,
mourning and weeping in this valley of tears.
Turn then, most gracious Advocate, thine eyes of mercy
toward us,
and after this our exile, show unto us
the blessed fruit of thy womb, Jesus,
O clement, O loving, O sweet Virgin Mary.

PRAYER TO THE HOLY SPIRIT

Come, Holy Spirit,
fill the hearts of thy faithful
and enkindle in them the fire of thy love.
Send forth thy Spirit, and they shall be created;
and Thou shalt renew the face of the earth.
Let Us Pray.
O God, who did instruct the Apostles by the light of the Holy
Spirit,
grant us in this same Spirit to be truly wise,
and ever rejoice in His consolation.
Through Christ our Lord.
Amen.

PRAYER TO ST. MICHAEL

Saint Michael, the Archangel, defend us in battle;
be our defense against the wickedness and snares of the devil.
May God rebuke him we humbly pray;
and do thou, 0 Prince of the heavenly host,
by the power of God, cast into hell
Satan and all the evil spirits who roam throughout the world
seeking the ruin of souls. Amen.

PRAYER BEFORE A CRUCIFIX

Good and sweetest Jesus, before Thy face I humbly kneel,
and with the greatest fervor of spirit I pray and beseech Thee
to fix deep in my heart lively sentiments of faith, hope, and
charity,
true sorrow for my sins and a firm purpose of amendment,
while I consider Thy five most Precious Wounds,
having before my eyes the words of David, the Prophet,
concerning Thee, my Jesus:
"They have pierced My hands and My feet,
they have numbered all My bones."

MORNING OFFERING

O Jesus, through the Immaculate Heart of Mary,
I offer Thee all my prayers, works, joys, and sufferings of this
day,
in union with the Holy Sacrifice of the Mass throughout the
world.
I offer them for all the intentions of your Sacred Heart:
the salvation of souls, reparation for sin, the reunion of all
Christians.
I offer them for the intentions of our Bishops, and all the
Apostles in Prayer,
and in particular for those recommended by our Holy Father
for this month.
Amen.

GRACE BEFORE MEALS

Bless us, 0 Lord, and these Thy gifts,
which we are about to receive from Thy bounty
through Christ, Our Lord. Amen.

GRACE AFTER MEALS

We give Thee thanks almighty God, for all Thy benefits;
Who livest and reignest, world without end.
May the souls of the faithful departed,
through the Mercy of God, rest in peace. Amen.

ACT OF FAITH

O my God, I firmly believe that thou are one God
in three Divine Persons: the Father, the Son, and the Holy
Spirit.
I believe that Thy Divine Son became man and died for our
sins,
and that He shall come to judge the living and the dead.
I believe these and all the truths which the Holy Catholic
Church teaches,
because Thou hast revealed them,
Who canst neither deceive nor be deceived. Amen.

ACT OF HOPE

O my God, relying on Thy almighty power and infinite mercy
and promises,
I hope to obtain the pardon of my sins with the help of Thy
grace,
and life everlasting, through the merits of Jesus Christ,
my Lord and my Redeemer. Amen.

ACT OF LOVE

O my God, I love Thee above all things
with my whole heart and soul,
because Thou are all good and deserving of all my love.
I love my neighbor as myself for the love of Thee.
I forgive all who have injured me and ask pardon
of all whom I have injured. Amen.

ACT OF CONTRITION

O my God, I am sorry for my sins with all my heart.
In choosing to do wrong, and failing to do good,
I have sinned against you, whom I love above all things.
With your grace, I will confess my sins,
do penance, and avoid the things that cause me to sin.
Your beloved Son Jesus suffered and died for me.
In His name, Dear Father, forgive my sins and have mercy on me.
Amen.

THE MYSTERIES OF THE ROSARY

Joyful Mysteries
The Annunciation
The Visitation
The Nativity
The Presentation
The Finding in the Temple

Sorrowful Mysteries
The Agony in the Garden
The Scourging at the Pillar
The Crowning with Thorns
The Carrying of the Cross
The Crucifixion

Glorious Mysteries
The Resurrection
The Ascension
The Decent of the Holy Spirit
The Assumption
The Coronation of Our Lady

FATIMA PRAYER

O my Jesus, forgive us our sins,
save us from the fires of hell,
lead all souls to heaven,
especially those who have most need of Thy mercy.

LAST PRAYER OF THE ROSARY

O God, Whose only begotten Son, by His life, death, and
resurrection
has purchased for us the rewards of eternal life,
grant, we beseech Thee, that meditating upon the mysteries
of the most Holy Rosary of the Blessed Virgin Mary,
we may imitate what they contain, and obtain what they
promise.
Through the same Christ our Lord. Amen.

THE DIVINE PRAISES

Blessed be God. Blessed Be His holy Name.
Blessed be Jesus Christ, true God and true Man.
Blessed be the name of Jesus. Blessed be His Most Sacred
Heart.
Blessed be His Most Sacred Blood.
Blessed be Jesus in the Most Holy Sacrament of the Altar.
Blessed be the great Mother of God, Mary most holy.
Blessed be her holy and Immaculate Conception.
Blessed be the name of Mary, Virgin and Mother.
Blessed be Saint Joseph, her most chaste Spouse.
Blessed be God in His Angels and In His Saints.

STATIONS OF THE CROSS

Jesus is condemned to death.
Jesus is made to carry His cross.
Jesus falls the first time.
Jesus meets His sorrowful mother.
Simon of Cyrene helps Jesus to carry His cross.
Veronica wipes the face of Jesus.
Jesus falls the second time.
The women of Jerusalem weep over Jesus.
Jesus falls the third time.
Jesus is stripped of His garments.
Jesus is nailed to the cross.
Jesus dies on the cross.
Jesus is taken down from the cross.
Jesus is laid in the tomb.

THE BEATITUDES

Blessed are the poor in spirit,
for theirs is the kingdom of heaven.
Blessed are the meek, for they shall possess the earth.
Blessed are they that mourn, for they shall be comforted.
Blessed are they that hunger and thirst after justice,
for they shall have their fill.
Blessed are the merciful, for they shall obtain mercy.
Blessed are the clean of heart, for they shall see God.
Blessed are the peacemakers, for they shall be called the
children of God.
Blessed are they that suffer persecution for justice' sake,
for theirs is the kingdom of heaven.

THE THREE THEOLOGICAL VIRTUES

Faith
Hope
Charity

THE FOUR CARDINAL VIRTUES

Prudence
Justice
Fortitude
Temperance

THE SEVEN CAPITAL SINS

Pride
Covetousness
Lust
Anger
Gluttony
Envy
Sloth

THE TWELVE APOSTLES

Simon Peter
Andrew
James the Greater
John
Philip
Bartholomew
Matthew
Thomas
James the Less
Simon the Zealot
Jude
Judas Iscariot
who was replaced by
Matthias

THE FOUR EVANGELISTS

St. Matthew
St. Mark
St. Luke
St. John

THE FOUR MARKS OF THE CHURCH

One
Holy
Catholic
Apostolic

THE TEN COMMANDMENTS

I am the Lord thy God. Thou shalt not have strange gods
before Me.
Thou shalt not take the name of the Lord thy God in vain.
Remember thou keep holy the Lord's day.
Honor thy father and thy mother.
Thou shalt not kill.
Thou shalt not commit adultery.
Thou shalt not steal.
Thou shalt not bear false witness against thy neighbor.
Thou shalt not covet thy neighbor's wife.
Thou shalt not covet thy neighbor's goods.

THE CHIEF SPIRITUAL WORKS OF MERCY

Admonish the sinner.
Instruct the ignorant.
Counsel the doubtful.
Comfort the sorrowful.
Bear wrongs patiently.
Forgive all injuries.
Pray for the living and the dead.

THE CHIEF CORPORAL WORKS OF MERCY

Feed the hungry.
Give drink to the thirsty.
Clothe the naked.
Shelter the homeless.
Visit the sick.
Visit the imprisoned.
Bury the dead.

FRUITS OF THE HOLY SPIRIT

Love
Joy
Peace
Patience
Goodness
Kindness
Gentleness
Faithfulness
Self-control

THE SEVEN GIFTS OF THE HOLY SPIRIT

Wisdom
Enables Christians to *recognize good* and to
know and appreciate what is of value to
those who live the Christian life.

Understanding
Helps Christians become aware of *how and where*
the Holy Spirit works within us and the Church.
It also helps us to be *sensitive* to one another.

Right Judgment
Helps Christians *make good decisions* in their own lives
and enables them to help others make good decisions.

Courage/Fortitude
Gives Christians *strength of character* so that they
can *act rightly and live* by Christian principles.

Knowledge
Enables Christians to *use wisely the intelligence*
that God has given them and to use their
gifts and talents to the fullest.

Piety/Reverence
Makes Christians *act lovingly* toward God
and all persons, places, and things related to God.

Holy Fear
of the Lord Helps Christians *acknowledge God's greatness*
and to avoid that which would offend God.

PRECEPTS OF THE CHURCH

To keep holy the day of the Lord's Resurrection:
To worship God by participating in Mass every Sunday
(or Saturday Vigil) and on holy days of obligation.
We are also to abstain from such work or business that
would inhibit the worship given to God, the joy proper
to the Lord's day, or due relaxation of mind and body.

To lead a sacramental life:
To receive Holy Communion frequently and the Sacrament of
Penance regularly. (Minimally – once a year)
(Holy Communion during the Paschal time unless for a good
reason this precept must be fulfilled during another
time of the year.)

**To study Catholic teaching in preparation for
Confirmation and to be confirmed.**

To observe the marriage laws of the Church:
To give religious training to one's children;
to use parish schools and religious education programs.

To strengthen and support the Church:
To support one's own parish community and parish priests,
the Church worldwide, and the Holy Father.

To do penance:
To abstain from meat and to fast on the appointed days.
Ash Wednesday and Good Friday – Fast and abstinence from
meat.
All Fridays during lent – Abstinence from meat.

To join in the missionary spirit of the Church:
Catholics belong to a worldwide community which has the
Lord's
own mandate to spread the good news. To this end, support
must be shown for the Pope and the missionary efforts
of the Church throughout the world.

HOLY DAYS OF OBLIGATION

Christmas Day (December 25)
Solemnity of Mary, Mother of God (January 1)
Ascension Thursday (40 days after Easter)
The Assumption (August 15)
All Saints' Day (November 1)
The Immaculate Conception (December 8)

References

Alberione, James, Reverend, S.S.P., S.T.D., **The Eternal Wisdom**, Boston, MA: Daughters of St. Paul, 1983.

A Team of Daughters of St. Paul, **His In The Spirit – Confirmation Program**, Boston, MA: Daughters of St. Paul, 1886.

Catechism of the Catholic Church, Libreria Editrice Vaticia, 1994.

Pennock, Michael Frances, **This Is Our Faith – A Catechism For Adults**, Notre Dame, IN: Ave Maria Press, 1989.

Stravinskas, Peter, M.J., Reverend, Ph.D., S.T.D., Editor. **Catholic Encyclopedia**, Huntington, IN: Our Sunday Visitor Publishing Division, Our Sunday Visitor, Inc., 1991.

St. Michael And The Angels, Compiled from Approved Sources, Rockford, IL: Tan Books and Publishers, Inc., 1983.

Willis, M.V., M.Ed., **Reclaiming Teenage Morality: Christian Ethics Vs. Modern Ethics.**, Vero Beach, FL: Ocean East Publishing, Inc., 1993.

Index

H

hatred 29, 60, 92, 107, 109, 111, 120
Hell 18, 25, 50, 140, 147
Holy Communion (see also Eucharist) 40, 43-44, 47-49, 51, 53, 59-60, 149, 167
holy day of obligation 108, 142, 167-168
Holy Sacrifice of the Mass 52, 107-108, 156
Holy Spirit 64, 81, 121, 138, 141, 143-144, 149, 151-153, 155, 157, 159, 166
Holy Water 96, 142
homosexuality 121
humility 48-49, 65, 93, 142

I

immoral 34, 119, 142, 146
impulsiveness 36, 142
Incarnation 27, 50, 86, 137, 142, 146
indifferentism 87

J

Jesus Christ 17-19, 27-28, 35, 39-40, 43-44, 47-53, 59-60, 63-65, 68, 78-79, 81, 86-87, 91-93, 95-97, 100, 104, 107, 109, 129, 131-132, 134, 137-138, 140-149, 152-161, 166, 168-169

L

lawful superiors 33, 143
liturgy 133, 143
love 24, 30, 32, 36, 51-53, 60, 85, 89-90, 93, 109, 110, 116-117, 119, 121, 124-125, 129, 132, 145, 153, 155, 158, 165
lust 28, 111, 113, 119-121, 144-143, 162

M

marital commitment 125
Mary 12, 17, 92, 95, 97, 103, 131-132, 142-143, 147-148, 152-154, 156, 160, 168
Mass 12, 34, 36-37, 52-53, 55, 59-60, 64, 86, 107-108, 140, 142, 156, 167

Michelle Willis

Jackie Cole

About the Authors

Michelle Willis holds a Masters Degree in Education and worked as a public school Health Educator from 1981 to 1995. Michelle is presently a Middle School Curriculum Coordinator. Since 1992 she has been the Director of Religious Education for St. John of the Cross Parish in Vero Beach, Florida, and holds a Professional Certificate in Catechesis from the Diocese of Palm Beach. Michelle's first book, *Reclaiming America's Children: Raising and Educating Morally Healthy Kids*, was published in 1991. A subsequent title, *Reclaiming Teenage Morality: Christian Ethics Vs. Modern Ethics*, was published in 1993.

Jackie Cole began her work in Religious Education in 1965 as a catechist. She is a former Early Childhood teacher. Her thirty years of teaching experience range from pre-school to adult education. Since 1984 she has been the Director of Religious Education and Youth Minister for Holy Cross Church in Vero Beach, Florida, and she holds a Professional Certificate in Catechesis from the Diocese of Palm Beach.

The authors have conducted numerous retreats and workshops for parents, teachers and students.

Reclaiming America's Children

by M. V. Willis

ISBN: 0-9607028-2-2
Category: Education
96 Pages
Trade Softcover
Price: $8.95

Public school health education teacher M. V. Willis draws on a decade of classroom experience to advise parents and teachers on the principles of discipline and how to handle the problems of disrespect, rebellion, impulsiveness, poor school performance, sexual promiscuity, drug abuse, and violence.

Reclaiming America's Children –

- Clearly defines and warns about recent controversial issues that affect children.
- Informs parents, teachers, and students about their rights and protections under federal law with reference to sex education, values education, and contradictory viewpoints in family, moral, ethical, and/or religious beliefs.
- Examines the influences of televised violence and sexually explicit rock music, music videos, and movies on young impressionable minds.
- Points out how adult magazines project violence, pornography, and the abuse of our children.

Reclaiming Teenage Morality

by M. V. Willis

ISBN: 0-9607028-3-0
Category: Education
151 Pages
Trade Softcover
Price: $8.95

An excellent resource for parents, teachers, pastors, youth ministers, religious education coordinators, and home schools.

Reclaiming Teenage Morality –

–   Explains how the moral revolution has changed people's ideas about sexual morality by overthrowing the authority of God and His moral laws.

–   Warns Christians about the subtle self-deception of professing belief in God while viewing God's moral laws as obsolete, nonexistent, or as a set of guidelines from which they can pick and choose.

–   Examines the influence of and exposes several dangerous and erroneous aspects of the New Age Movement.

–   Points out the importance of a properly formed conscience and its role in the development of a strong Christian character.

- Exposes the "hidden agenda" of humanistic values education and sex education programs.

- Stresses the importance of making decisions based on God's revealed moral laws, the Gospel of Jesus Christ, and teachings of Christ's Church.

- Emphasizes the importance of keeping God's commandments based on Jesus' promise to acknowledge faithfulness to His commandments as a sign of one's love for Him.

Reclaiming Teenage Morality is designed to be read individually or to be used as the text for a course. Those who want to utilize *Reclaiming Teenage Morality* as a text may order –

Reclaiming Teenage Morality: Christian Ethics Vs. Modern Ethics Teacher Curriculum Resource Kit

Each Teacher Curriculum Resource Kit Contains These Items.

◆ A Teacher Curriculum Guide with the following features:
  - Suggested Teaching Sequence
  - Chapter Objectives
  - Copy-Ready Worksheets with Answer Keys
  - Activity Guides
  - Suggested Supplemental Teaching Aids
  - Suggestions for Audio-Visual Supplementation

◆ A copy of *RECLAIMING TEENAGE MORALITY: Christian Ethics vs. Modern Ethics*
◆ A copy of *RECLAIMING AMERICA'S CHILDREN: Raising and Educating Morally Healthy Kids*

See the page 187 for ordering information.

THE SCORPION FILES
TEACHER CURRICULUM RESOURCE KIT

The Scorpion Files is designed to be read individually or to be used as the text for a course. Those who want to utilize *The Scorpion Files* as a text may order *The Scorpion Files: Teacher Curriculum Resource Kit*.

Each Teacher Curriculum Resource Kit contains these items.

- A Teacher Curriculum Guide with the following features:
  - Copy-Ready Worksheets with Answer Keys
    Terms To Know
    Getting the Facts
    Asking Ourselves Why
  - Copy-Ready Reflection/Journal Pages
- A copy of *THE SCORPION FILES: Lies Satan Tells to Young Catholics*
- A copy of *RECLAIMING AMERICA'S CHILDREN: Raising and Educating Morally Healthy Kids*
- A copy of *RECLAIMING TEENAGE MORALITY: Christian Ethics vs. Modern Ethics*

See page 187 for ordering information.

ORDER FORM

Ocean East Publishing
1655 - 71st Court
Vero Beach, Florida 32966

Phone (561) 567-9996   Fax (561) 567-8872

Name: ____

Address: ____

City: ____

State: ________________________________ Zip: ___________

Reclaiming America's Children
ISBN: 0-9607028-2-2 (see page 181)
_____ copies @ $8.95 each = $ ___________________ *

Reclaiming Teenage Morality
ISBN: 0-9607028-3-0 (see page 182)
_____ copies @ $8.95 each = $ ___________________ **

Relaiming Teenage Morality:
Teacher's Curriculum Resource Kit
ISBN: 0-9607028-4-9 (see page 183)
_____ copies @ $47.50 each = $ ___________________ **

The Scorpion Files
ISBN: 0-9607028-5-7
_____ copies @ $12.00 each = $ ___________________

The Scorpion Files:
Teacher Curriculum Resource Kit
ISBN: 0-9607028-6-5
_____ copies @ $62.00 each = $ ___________________

Subtotal . . . . $ ___________________

Sales Tax (Add 7%) . . . . $ ___________________

Shipping and Handling ($4.50 for first book/
$1 for each additional book) . . . . $ ___________________

Total . . . . . . $ ___________________

Make all checks payable to **Ocean East Publishing.**
Visa/MasterCard Available.